# *The Secondhand Basenji Ha...*

## The Guide to Adopting and Living with a "Rescued" Basenji

Written & Photographed by Patrick J. Cotter & Maria Cotter

Revised & Expanded Second Edition: July, 1999

**Windigo**

# *The Secondhand Basenji Handbook*
## The Guide to Adopting and Living with a "Rescued" Basenji
### Revised & Expanded Second Edition: July, 1999

ISBN 0-9658488-1-7
Printed and bound in the United States of America.

**Windigo**

E-mail inquiries may be sent to:
info@windigo.net

P.O. Box 183176
Shelby Township, MI 48318-3176

The Windigo web site address is:
http://www.windigo.net

The advice contained in this publication is based solely on the opinions of the authors. This publication is designed to be an informative guide in regards to the subject matter covered. It is provided with the understanding that the publisher/authors are not engaged in rendering veterinary, behavioral, legal, or other professional services. Where professional services are required, the services of a competent professional person should be sought.

# *Acknowledgements*

The authors would like to thank the following folks for their contributions:

☞ All of the readers and rescue contacts who provided feedback on the first edition of *The Secondhand Basenji Handbook* and therefore helped to make this second edition even more comprehensive.

☞ Sally Wallis, of Zande Basenjis in England, for granting us permission to use the extensive "Ongoing Basenji Bibliography" as we updated and improved Appendix A of this handbook.

☞ Mike Swan for providing us with information on the wonderful work done by Basenji Rescue and Transport, Inc. (BRAT) and the Basenji Underground Railroad, included in the Tailtip after Section 4 of this handbook, and for allowing us to print the rescue application and adoption contract from the BRAT web site as examples in Section 5.

☞ The Basenji Club of Greater Detroit for facilitating our involvement in Basenji rescue, and for allowing us to have a positive impact on the lives of many of the rescues pictured in this handbook.

Finally, we'd be remiss if we didn't mention the lucky rescue Basenjis and their owners whose photograph graces the next page and back cover. They are, from left to right standing: Dan Baker and Jeff Kast with their rescued Basenji Toby; Gary and Julie Ankers with their rescued Basenji Arrow; and Janet Onderchanin and Ron Bright with their rescued Basenji Windsor. From left to right kneeling they are: Charmaine Ziegeler with her rescued Basenji Callie; and Jim and Sue LaBean with their rescued Basenji Magic. The photograph was taken at a Fun Match & Rescue Reunion sponsored by the Basenji Club of Greater Detroit in the Fall of 1997.

*Thanks!*

# Table of Contents

# *Table of Contents (Continued)*

# *Foreword*

One of my very best friends when I was growing up in northern Indiana was a dog that our neighbors had "rescued." One cold snowy morning they found a young dog almost frozen to death in a snowbank at the end of their driveway. No one ever came forward to claim her, so her true heritage was never known. Duchess grew well and strong under her rescuers' care, and when she and I met we were destined to become great friends. Even after my family and I moved to Michigan, I never forgot Duchess or the fun times we shared.

I had the opportunity to visit her a few years later, and she greeted me with all the enthusiasm and happiness that I had hoped she would. This picture of us was taken that day we were reunited. We didn't know it then, but it was the last time we were to ever be together. A few years ago Duchess left this world, but her spirit remains with me still. What a friend I would have missed, had she not been rescued.

It's Duchess' spirit that keeps the rescue flame alive in me, and it's the spirit of the rescue Basenjis I've known that makes a hard job like rescue a commitment I feel so passionately about. It's not just the Basenji folks dedicated to rescue, but all people and organizations who are involved in some way with rescue efforts that are giving "second chances" to dogs every day, year after year. Without these folks doing this hard task, imagine what friends so many adoptive families would be missing.

My experience with Basenji rescue has been extremely rewarding. I've been asked many times if it's hard to let the dogs go when it's time for their adoption, and my response is yes, it's hard to see them go, because I love them all so very much. But I know that when they go home to their new families, I have done everything I possibly can to make sure their new homes are the homes in which they'll live out the remainder of their days. Knowing you've been instrumental in making a difference, knowing that you've given these rescues a "second chance" at life, is a joy that makes doing rescue all worthwhile. If I'd never done rescue, I sure would've missed out on some wonderful friends!

*Maria Cotter*
*July, 1996*

*This handbook is dedicated
to the memory of Duchess,
to the Basenjis we've "rescued,"
and to all rescued Basenjis
and their rescuers.*

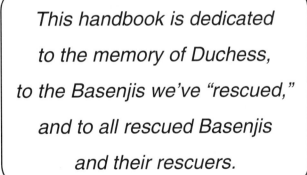

*We'd also like to devote this handbook to the newest member of our family,
our beautiful daughter Ellie,
and to the Basenjis that currently share our lives —
Chumba (Windigo's Mr. Happy Go Lucky),
Kaya (Ch. Dedela Kaya M'Ntanami Cotter),
and Buddy (Ch. Windigo's Sunfire of Kazanya).*

# *Introduction*

You're thinking about adding a Basenji to your family, and you're considering adopting a "rescued" Basenji. Good for you!

Welcome to the second edition of *The Secondhand Basenji Handbook.*

Basenjis as a breed have a long and colorful history. Through the centuries they've been beloved companions of pharaohs, kings, hunters in the African bush — and of ordinary people like you and me.

Basenjis are remarkable, intelligent, and challenging — but they're not for everyone. If you have patience, lots of love to share and a good sense of humor, you already have three of the basic tools you'll need to share your life with a Basenji! But a Basenji, just like any other breed of dog, is a lifelong commitment. You'll want to be absolutely sure a Basenji is right for you before you purchase or adopt one.

That's where this handbook comes in. *The Secondhand Basenji Handbook* is designed to help you decide if a "rescued" Basenji is right for you. It starts with the basics — answers to some frequently asked questions about Basenjis — in Section 1. In Section 2, we define "rescue" and introduce you to the world of rescue work: the dogs, the people and the process. In the next section, Section 3, we'll tell you what to look for in a rescue group, and what to avoid.

We've included some of the questions the rescue people may ask you in Section 4 — along with the reasons those questions are asked, and we've also provided some questions you may want to ask of any rescue group you're considering adopting a dog from. Section 5 of this handbook has a sample adoption application and contract.

The information in Section 6 will help guide you if you're considering adopting a Basenji from an animal shelter or humane society, and children and dogs are the topic of Section 7.

Section 8 will assist you as you plan and prepare for the arrival of your new Basenji, and it includes a shopping list for your convenience! In Section 9, we tell you a few things to keep in mind as you welcome your Basenji home, and you'll find some tips on making your new life together a success in Section 10.

We all make mistakes sometimes, and Section 11 talks about some common mistakes you'll want to avoid to help make your rescue experience a success. If you're having problems with your Basenji, Section 12 might provide some helpful advice for dealing with those issues.

Of course, you'll want to keep your Basenji "running right," so Section 13 provides some guidelines for caring for your Basenji and keeping him healthy.

In the last section of this handbook, Section 14, you'll find stories about rescued Basenjis, the people who adopted them, and their adoption experiences. What better way to hear about the successes of rescue than to hear from people who have adopted Basenjis!

Between the sections of this handbook we've included helpful hints and discussions we've dubbed "Tailtips." Tailtips will provide you with information on things such as crates, riding in the car with your Basenji, and healthy treat ideas.

You'll find four Appendices at the back of this handbook. Appendix A will give you information on Basenji-related publications. In Appendix B, we've included a rescue group contact log to help you keep track of people you talk to, and there's a shopping list in Appendix C you can take with you when you're ready to prepare for your rescue's arrival. Finally, Appendix D gives you some space to record information about your Basenji.

If you do your homework, adopting a rescue Basenji can prove to be a rewarding experience for you, and you will have given a homeless dog a new chance at a wonderful life.

We encourage you to learn as much about Basenjis as you can before you decide whether you'll adopt one, and we hope this handbook will be a valuable resource for you. Good luck!

# Section 1.  Common Questions People Ask About Basenjis — and the Answers

There are many excellent reference books on the market today about Basenjis, and you'll find a list of them in Appendix A. These books are a good place to start your research on Basenjis. They will provide you with breed history, the breed standard, and a good general overview of what the Basenji breed is all about. We don't want to repeat the information that these books contain, but this section does provide the answers to some common questions that people ask about Basenjis. If you would like to know more about the breed, we suggest you refer to any of the reference books listed in Appendix A. Of course, another good source of information is other Basenji owners!

The importance of learning about the breed via books, talking with Basenji owners, rescue groups, and clubs is that you can show you've done your homework. You'll have a good working knowledge of the breed, and you'll have more realistic expectations about Basenjis. Most importantly, you'll discover whether or not a Basenji is the right breed for you.

**Q: What is a Basenji?**

**A:** The Basenji, popularly known as the "barkless" dog, is one of the oldest breeds. Basenjis were highly valued hunting dogs of some native African tribes. Basenjis are sighthounds, bred to be independent, resourceful, and efficient hunters.

**Q: So if Basenjis are "barkless," then they don't make noise, right?**

**A:** Wrong! Although Basenjis are called "barkless," they are not totally mute. They can make the usual "doggy" noises such as growling, whining, and yelping, plus they have their own special noise. This special noise can be described as a mixture between a chortle and a yodel. Basenjis can also scream and howl.

**Q: How big do Basenjis get?**

**A:** The Basenji is a small, lightly built dog. According to the American Kennel Club (AKC) breed standard, the ideal height for males is 17 inches (43 cm) at the shoulder, and for females it's 16 inches (41 cm). Males are about 17 (43 cm) inches from the front of the chest to the point of the buttocks, and females are about 16 inches (41 cm). The approximate weight is 24 pounds (11 kg) for males and 22 pounds (10 kg) for females.

**Q: What colors do Basenjis come in?**

**A:** Basenjis come in four colors that are recognized by the American Kennel Club (AKC): red & white; black & white; black, tan & white (known as tricolor); and brindle & white. All color variations have four white feet, a white chest, and a white tailtip. White can be present on the face, neck, and underparts of the Basenji, but it doesn't have to be. All Basenjis have an expressive, wrinkled forehead.

**Q: What kind of pets do Basenjis make?**

**A:** Basenjis are not for everyone. The first impression

one gets of a Basenji is that he is a proud little dog. Much of the Basenji's charm lies in its individuality and extreme intelligence. Although affectionate, the Basenji does not overdo its devotion; there is just too much curiosity in its makeup. Everything has to be examined and inquired into, which makes the Basenji a wonderful companion, but not an over-obedient one. Basenjis are very intelligent, but they can get bored easily. While finding ways to entertain themselves, they can get into lots of trouble!

**Q: What times of the year are Basenji puppies usually available?**

**A:** Most Basenji females come into season once a year, usually during late fall. This means that Basenji puppies are generally available in late December and January. However, some females come into season earlier, and some have seasons twice a year. You'll sometimes find puppies available in the summer and early fall.

**Q: How long do Basenjis live?**

**A:** Basenjis can live to be 10 to 15 years of age. This means that your Basenji will most likely be around for a long time, so it's important that you do your homework. Researching the breed and talking with Basenji owners will help you make sure a Basenji is right for you *before* you make your decision to adopt or purchase one.

**Q: What sorts of health problems can Basenjis develop?**

**A:** Like most breeds, Basenjis can have a few genetic health problems, and breeders need to be careful about checking breeding stock. Some diseases that can affect Basenjis are Hemolytic Anemia (HA), Hip Dysplasia, Fanconi Syndrome, Persistent Pupillary Membrane (PPM), and Progressive Retinal Atrophy (PRA). Some of these diseases can be avoided, but some cannot. For more details on these and other genetic diseases that can affect Basenjis, talk to your veterinarian and to Basenji breeders. You can also learn more by reading some of the reference books listed in Appendix A.

**Q: Are Basenjis good with children?**

**A:** Basenjis are usually good around children. However, it's important to supervise your children around *any* breed of dog. Teach your children how to properly meet and play with dogs, and keep in mind that your Basenji enjoys and needs quiet time as well as fun and games. See Section 7 of this handbook, "Children and Dogs: Knowing the Rules," for more information on children and dogs.

**Q: Do Basenjis need a lot of exercise?**

**A:** Basenjis are often described as a bundle of energy in a small package. They require more than just a daily walk in order to remain healthy and fit. People who enjoy outdoor activities, such as running or walking, often discover that their Basenjis enjoy these activities too!

**Q: I work during the day. Can I leave my Basenji loose in my home?**

**A:** Basenjis can be mischievous and easily bored. It can be a big mistake to leave an untrained Basenji alone in your home. They can be extremely destructive if left to entertain themselves. If you're going to leave your Basenji home alone, the safest and best place for it is in its crate.

**Q: Is the Basenji the kind of dog I can let off leash?**

**A:** *All* dogs should be contained in a fenced-in yard or kennel run, rather than being allowed to run loose. Basenjis are sighthounds and love to run. If allowed off leash, they will chase anything that moves. Unfortunately, they believe they can outrun any danger. Underground "radio-type" fencing does not work well with Basenjis, either. *If you want a dog that you can allow to run free, then you don't want a Basenji.*

**Q: I have allergies, and I've heard that Basenjis are non-allergenic. Is this true?**

**A:** No matter what people may tell you, *there is no breed of dog that is completely non-allergenic.* However, many people with allergies find that they can live with a Basenji because Basenjis have a short coat and lack a "doggy" odor. If you have allergies, it's a good idea to spend some time around Basenjis before you make the commitment to purchase or adopt one.

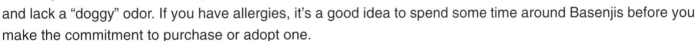

**Q: I've heard that Basenjis are "indoor" dogs. Is this true?**

**A:** Yes. Because of their short coat and minimal body fat, Basenjis are not suited to living outdoors, especially in climates that have rainy, snowy, or cold seasons. Basenjis prefer warm and dry places (and the company of their owners!), and you'll find that they'll seek out the sunny spot by a window or claim a place directly over a heat duct! In warmer seasons, Basenjis like to be outdoors and do enjoy the sunshine, but they need access to shade and fresh water at all times. Unless you live where it's warm year-round, the best place for your Basenji to live is indoors. Another thing to keep in mind is that Basenjis, like all dogs, are pack animals, and they want to be where the action is — with you! Also, leaving your Basenji outdoors unattended for long periods of time may lead to boredom and bad habits like digging and fence-climbing, and it makes him an easy target for dog thieves.

## *Tailtip – Canine Security Systems: Protecting Your Dog from Loss and Theft*

Think back to the last time you saw a "LOST DOG" sign — it probably wasn't very long ago. Many people are complacent about the safety of their dog, until the dog is accidentally lost or stolen. The sad part is that many of these lost pets end up euthanized in animal shelters, or worse, sold to research laboratories — simply because their owners could not be located. The technology we have available to us today makes it almost inexcusable for pets to be unprotected. *Every* pet should be protected against loss and theft, and there are many ways to do just that.

Perhaps the simplest way to protect your dog is also the most inexpensive — with a collar and identification tags. A sturdy nylon or leather collar is best. You'll have your choice of the conventional buckle design, the plastic fastener design, or a martingale-type collar. Either way, you'll want the collar to be just the right size for your dog. (You should be able to get two fingers between the collar and your dog's neck.)

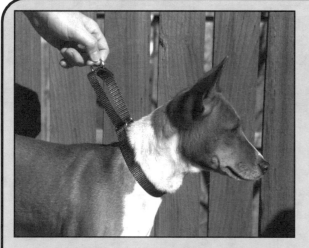

Keep in mind that while the plastic fastener-type collars are easier to get on and off your dog, they can and do sometimes come apart under stress. If your dog pulls on his leash when you walk, you'll probably want to stick with a buckle collar or a martingale-type collar (shown at left) that is designed to slip over the dog's head. You may want to use the plastic fastener-type collar only when your dog will be out in his yard. You don't ever want to leave any sort of choke collar on your dog, especially when he's unattended. It's too easy for him to get the collar hooked onto something and strangle.

Your dog's collar (or collars) should also sport an identification tag and a current dog license. The identification tag should include your last name, address, and a phone number where you can be reached. If space permits, you may also be able to add an additional phone number of a friend who can take the dog if you are unable to be reached. If your dog is tattooed or microchipped, you can include the name and phone number of the registry on the identification tag, along with a message like "I am tattooed" or "I am microchipped." Some types of nylon and leather collars can also be personalized with your information by monogramming.

It's a good idea to have your dog wear his collar and identification tags whenever possible — except while he's in his crate. It's too easy for a collar or tag to get hung up on the crate. Your dog could be injured or strangled if this happens. There are also collars available today that allow you to record a message (your name, address, phone number, etc.) into an electronic box attached to the collar!

Collars and tags are a great way to protect your dog, but they are only the first line of defense. The problem with collars and tags is that they can and do fall off, and it's too easy for a thief to simply remove them. Your second line of defense is a more permanent one, and that's tattooing and microchipping.

Tattooing is a great way to identify your pet because a tattoo is simple, painless, easy to apply, and lasts your dog a lifetime. In fact, many rescue groups tattoo the dogs they place, and the dog you adopt may already be tattooed! The tattoo itself is a series of numbers and letters that's unique to your dog. For example, many people use the last four digits of their Social Security number plus one additional letter or number. Rescue groups that tattoo often have a special sequence of numbers and letters which indicates that the dog came from their rescue group.

One myth about tattoos is that they are only for "valuable" show dogs. That's simply not true! Any dog can be tattooed, and the most important thing to keep in mind is that in order for a tattoo to be effective, it must be registered with a regional or national registry. In the United States, it's a violation of Federal law for research laboratories to use tattooed pets for research — a real plus for your pet. And, because tattoos cannot be removed, your pet is always protected, even if he isn't wearing his collar and tags.

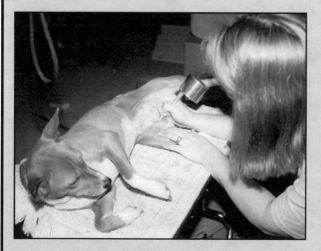

You can expect to pay between $10 and $15 to have a tattoo done, and you can also expect a $25 to $40 charge to register the tattoo with a registry. A tattoo should never, ever be done on your dog's ear (thieves have been known to cut an ear off just to remove a tattoo!). The best place is the inside part of a rear leg. Most dogs don't object to getting tattooed at all — in fact, all they usually feel is a gentle "tickle" from the tattoo marker. The dogs that do object to the tattoo process are usually frightened by the buzzing of the tattoo marker, or they aren't used to being made to lie down on one side.

Often, breed clubs hold tattoo clinics as fund-raisers — it shouldn't be too hard to find someone to do the tattoo for your dog. Another thing to remember about tattoos is that most people are familiar with tattoos on dogs, and shelters routinely check the dogs that arrive for tattoos.

Now, some folks don't like the idea of their dog being "marked" with a tattoo, and instead opt to have their dog microchipped. Some rescue groups implant the dogs they place with a microchip. The microchip itself is a bit larger than a grain of rice, and it's encased in a protective capsule. It's injected with a needle under the skin of your dog, usually between the shoulder blades. Once a microchip is implanted, a special hand-held scanner is used to read the code on the microchip. Once it's in your dog, you can't see the microchip at all — in fact, the only way to tell it's there is with a special scanner. If you're interested in having your dog microchipped, you may find that in your area only a veterinarian can do the implant. While it only takes a moment to implant the chip, your dog may feel some discomfort from the rather large needle.

If your dog doesn't like getting shots, then he probably won't like getting the microchip implanted. The "plus" side to microchips is also their "down" side — you can't tell that the microchip is there without using a scanner. There are several companies marketing their own brand of microchip, as well as their own special hand-held scanners. The problem is that not all scanners scan all types of microchips — some scanners may not pick up the presence of a microchip at all, while others can detect it's presence but can't give you the information off the microchip.

The other down side to microchips is that, no matter what people claim, they have a tendency to travel from the point of implant. Microchips implanted between the shoulders have been known to travel to the legs, knees, and feet of dogs. If you do get your dog microchipped, carefully follow the veterinarian's instructions on keeping your dog quiet and immobile for the time specified to help prevent the microchip from traveling.

While most people aren't familiar with microchips for dog identification, more and more shelters routinely scan dogs for them. Contact your veterinarian for more information on microchipping. In the U.S. you can expect to pay between $10 and $40 to have your dog microchipped, and you can expect to pay about $25 to $40 to register the microchip with a registry. Just like with tattoos, microchips are useless unless they are registered with a regional or national registry. If you decide to have your dog microchipped, you may also want to consider tattooing your dog as a "backup." That way, if the microchip has traveled or the scanner someone is using isn't compatible with your dog's microchip, your dog can still be identified by his tattoo.

# Section 2. "Rescue" Defined

The purpose of rescue is to find to new and loving homes for unwanted dogs. Rescue work may be done by groups or privately by individuals who have an interest in saving dogs. Rescue is often supported by national and local breed clubs. In fact, there are even organizations solely dedicated to rescue work.

Doing rescue work is difficult, and it can be heartbreaking. Sometimes a Basenji is rescued from a terrible situation and must be put to sleep, simply because someone has been so terribly cruel to it that it can't be rehabilitated. Other times, the Basenjis are abandoned by their owners because the dogs simply grew too old and required too much care.

Rescue work can be extremely demanding because what a rescuer is doing, in effect, is taking responsibility for a dog who's owner can no longer care for him or simply doesn't want him anymore. The rescue person provides shelter, food and basic care for the dog. In the meantime, as they get to know the dog, the rescuer evaluates him and decides what kind of home would be best for the dog. Rescuers also work to rehabilitate and train dogs who may need some behavioral modifications before they'll be ready for new homes. The reward for doing breed rescue comes when a match is made and the rescued dog becomes part of a loving family. That's the goal of breed rescue.

Just as there are a multitude of stars in the sky, there are a multitude of reasons why people give up their Basenjis (or any other breed of dog, for that matter). Some dogs are given up because a new baby has arrived and the new parents don't seem to have the time they once did for the dog. Others are given up because their owners impulsively purchased a cute little puppy from a pet store or a backyard breeder, only to find that it has grown up into a completely different adult dog. Rarely will you find puppies or Basenjis less than one year old in rescue. Other Basenjis end up in rescue due to their owners' deaths, job changes that force relocation, and divorces. Some dogs are even rescued off the streets or out of animal shelters — let loose by their owners and left to fend for themselves.

The list of reasons is endless, but the fact remains that with a lack of a public educated on the breed and with the continuance of puppy mills and disreputable breeders, breed rescue remains a busy job for those of us who love Basenjis.

The vast majority of the Basenjis that end up in rescue aren't bad dogs at all. You can't blame the dog if the owner didn't take the time to properly train it, care for it, or give it the attention and love it needs. You can't blame the owner either if something unforeseen happened and the dog ended up displaced.

Basenjis are very intelligent dogs, and they learn quickly what they can and can't get away with. Many first-time Basenji owners feel that this is too great a challenge, and if you've talked at length to Basenji owners, you will understand what this means. Every breed of dog — every individual dog, for that matter — has its particular idiosyncrasies, and Basenjis just happen to be a bit more challenging than some of the more popular breeds.

Breed rescue is not simply a matter of getting a dog and finding it a new home. Breed rescue involves finding out as much history on the dog as possible, evaluating the dog in a variety of social situations with various ages of children and adults, and determining what type of home environment the dog will fit in best.

Also, part of the rescue process is the everyday care involved, such as feeding, exercise, training, visits to the vet, and lots of love and attention. Rescuers spend a lot of time evaluating prospective new homes and owners. If a match is found and a dog is adopted, rescue people continue to be involved by providing follow-up phone calls and visits, and they are there to answer any questions that the family may have about their new dog.

Unfortunately, not all breed clubs support rescue. Some clubs don't have enough members interested or able to do rescue, or they don't have the funds required, and some clubs simply choose not to. Individuals as well as clubs do breed rescue, and if you are interested in adopting a Basenji through rescue, there are some things you need to know. The next section will tell you all about rescue groups — what to look for, and what to avoid.

## *Tailtip – Rescued Treasures*

As any dog lover would agree, there's nothing sweeter than the gentle *whuffs* of puppy breath against your skin. If you've ever cradled a day-old pup in the palm of your hand, you'll understand the awesome miracle of that new little life. You do, quite literally, hold in your hand a creature of great promise, whose entire life will be shaped by its daily experiences and the people it meets from its birth day forward. If it's a lucky pup, it will find a safe and secure home with people who will respect, treasure, train, and love it unconditionally for its entire life.

If it's not one of the lucky ones, though, life can be a tough struggle with few kindnesses and rewards. Even for beloved pets whose owners no longer can keep them and must relinquish them to rescue, the shock of losing their "family" can be a great stress on a heart and soul who once thought there was only one place to ever call home.

Without the benefit of dedicated rescuers, dogs might never be given a second chance. Therein lies the reward in doing rescue work (and in adopting a rescue dog) — knowing that you've helped dogs who may have had a hard start in life find their way to loving, permanent homes and rewarding lives.

Certainly, as sweet as puppy breath can be, if you've ever gazed into the eyes of a rescued dog and found happiness, contentment, and love staring right back, you'll understand the awesome miracle of that *rescued* life. You have before you a creature of great promise, whose life will continue to be shaped by its daily experiences and the people it meets from its rescue day forward. Lucky to be in a safe and secure home with people who will respect, treasure, train and love it unconditionally for the remainder of its life, the rescued dog appears to remember where it's been and seems especially grateful for it's new home and new family.

Do they remember their old lives, and awaken from dreams wondering for the briefest moment if their happiness was only imagined? Do they lay awake in the darkness, or perhaps doze in a sunlit corner, listening as their new people move through life, hearing voices and laughter, and knowing that they've found home again? Perhaps they do these things, the rescued treasures, and perhaps they don't. We'll never know for certain. But one thing we do know is that being rescued and given a second chance is a wonderful gift that keeps on giving!

## Section 3. Rescue Groups: What to Look for and What to Avoid

Finding a rescue organization in your area might require a bit of searching on your part. The odds of finding one listed in the Yellow Pages are pretty slim, so you need to be clever in your search. You can start by contacting the Basenji Club of America (BCOA) or your local Basenji club. If there's someone who does rescue in your area, the BCOA or your local club will be able to direct you to them. For those of you who have Internet access, the Basenji Rescue and Transport, Inc. (BRAT) web site is an excellent resource, and the BCOA has a web site, too — see "Basenjis on the Internet" in Appendix A of this handbook for the web site address. (For more information about BRAT, see the Tailtip after Section 4 in this handbook.) In some cases, there may not be any rescue groups or individuals in your area, but don't be discouraged. Many rescue groups will gladly work with you, even if you don't live in their areas.

Another place you may want to check is the classified section of your local paper. Often rescue groups hold fun matches and clinics, or they may advertise if they have dogs available for adoption. Visit your local pet store, and you may find business cards, a poster, or flyers advertising breed rescue.

Dog shows are another good place to find out about rescues. Talk with other Basenji fanciers at these shows, but please wait until they have shown their dogs and breed judging is complete! Purchase a show catalog. In the show catalog you will find the names and addresses of Basenji breeders and exhibitors who may be able to help you locate a rescue group.

What you want to find is a rescue group or person who has their "act together." This means that they have established guidelines for screening and accepting dogs for rescue, and guidelines for placing them. They have a standardized adoption application, and may have a simple handout or brochure that describes the breed. They have a process for screening applicants, and they ask a reasonable adoption fee for the dogs they place. They will insist on the rescue dog being spayed or neutered before adoption or shortly thereafter, and they will take the time to follow up with phone calls, home visits and whatever else is necessary to ensure that the placement works out. And, they are available to answer any questions you may have. A rescue group that has its act together will try very hard to find the right home for the right dog. Knowing that the rescue group has guidelines and rules helps ensure that the dog you adopt is the right dog for you.

Be wary of any rescue group or person that tries to place a dog quickly and doesn't take the time to find out much about you. Avoid giving *anyone* any money up front to "hold a dog." Reputable rescue groups don't take any money for a dog until they have screened you, and are ready to place the dog with you. The rescue group that quotes you one adoption fee should not raise it once it has been quoted, unless they have a very good reason for doing so.

There isn't any money to be made in rescue work, and you should be on guard if anyone seems to be asking too high a price. Usually, the price that a rescue group charges for an adoption fee is considerably less than what you'd pay for a puppy. Money from the adoption fee goes to pay for expenses, such as vet visits, spaying or neutering, tattooing or microchipping, and any other expenses the rescue group has incurred while the dog was in their care.

Don't be afraid to ask a lot of questions about the rescue or rescues you are interested in. No question is a stupid question, and you have the right to know what you are getting before you get it. See Section 4 in this book for more information on questions you'll want to ask. Also, you should be able to visit the home of the rescue person and see where the dogs are kept. If someone won't let you visit, find yourself another rescue group to deal with. The basic rule of thumb is that if something doesn't seem right, it probably isn't.

When you contact a member of a rescue group, remember that people who do breed rescue are just like you and me — they work, have small children, etc. — they have lives! Be courteous and wait until after 10:00 before calling in the morning, and don't call after 9:00 at night. Often, rescue people are also dog show people, so don't expect them to answer the phone on Saturday or Sunday!

When you leave a message, be sure to speak clearly, tell them where you got their name and number, and that you are interested in adopting a rescue Basenji. Also — be patient! It may take a day or so for the person to get back with you. You may want to contact several different rescue groups.

When you do get a call back, expect to be asked some questions about why you are interested in the breed, why you would like to adopt, etc. The rescue person may or may not have dogs available for placement. If they do, they should be able to tell you about the dogs they have. They also may want to send you an adoption application and questionnaire, as well as some general breed information.   They may have even given you this handbook to read! They'll be able to tell right away whether or not you've done your homework on researching the breed, and the more you are able to show them that you *have* done your homework, the better off you'll be.

## *Tailtip – Bring on the Basenjis! Getting Involved with Basenji Rescue*

Do you love dogs? Do you have a special place in your heart just for Basenjis? Then you should consider getting involved with Basenji rescue! Being involved doesn't necessarily mean you'll have to take in dogs. In fact, there are many facets to rescue work, so it shouldn't be too much of a stretch for you to find something that matches your interests and abilities!

The best way to get involved with rescue work is to start by joining a local and/or national Basenji club, such as the Basenji Club of America (BCOA). Basenji clubs usually sponsor some kind of rescue work, so you can learn about rescue and meet club members involved in rescue by attending club meetings and events. There are also other rescue organizations — like Basenji Rescue and Transport, Inc. (BRAT) in the U.S.A. — that you can join. You can get information on joining the BCOA and BRAT at their web sites. See "Basenjis on the Internet" in Appendix A of this handbook for the web site addresses. Basenji clubs and rescue organizations offer many opportunities for you to become involved with Basenji rescue.

Become an active member, get to know the people in the club, and take the time to learn all you can about the breed. No matter how you decide to help out, your assistance will be greatly appreciated!

Here are some of the ways you can be involved in Basenji rescue:

**Foster Care**

Simply put, foster care is all about taking care of rescued Basenjis. When you foster a rescue, the dog lives with you, and you're responsible for its everyday care and for any special care it may need.

You'll also be responsible for getting to know the dog — it's personality, how much training it has had, and how it acts around children, adults, and other pets. While the dog is in your care, you may need to work to train it, rehabilitate it, and socialize it, too.

If you decide you'd like to foster a rescue, here are a few things you'll want to keep in mind:

- **Local laws and zoning ordinances.** It's a good idea to obtain copies of the local laws and ordinances pertaining to dogs. Many times there are strict rules regarding how many adult dogs you can have on your premises. You may also discover there are rules requiring the licensing of individuals who handle these dogs, as well as licensing of the dogs themselves.

- **Your family.** Do you have small children? Unless your children are old enough to be thoroughly trusted around dogs, and unless you're willing to supervise your children every minute when they're with a new dog, you shouldn't get involved with foster care. A large part of fostering involves getting to know the rescue's personality — if a dog didn't get along with the children in his previous home, he probably will have difficulty adjusting to yours. Also, you'll want to make sure that fostering a dog is fine with all the other people you live with.

- **Your pets.** Do you have a dog? Other pets? If you do, you'll want to consider the ramifications of bringing in a foster dog. You are most familiar with your pets — will they accept a new dog in the house? If you have a dog, is he crate trained? Has he had some basic obedience training? If you have a cat, does it have claws or have the claws been removed? Are any of your pets very old or very young? Are they in excellent health? Know what the tolerances and limitations of your current pets are, and then you'll be able to decide if you can safely bring in a rescue.

- **Your home.** If you have pets, you'll need to keep the foster dog separate from them for at least a week (or perhaps longer if a veterinarian deems it necessary). You need to be sure that the new dog is free of diseases and parasites before allowing him to mingle with the rest of your crew. Do you have the facilities to keep the new dog in isolation for observation? Is your yard fenced? Can you provide a "potty area" for the foster dog that is separate from your dogs' area? Where will the foster dog live, eat and sleep?

- **Your time.** Today it seems that we have so much to do and so little time to do it. If you're thinking about fostering a Basenji, take a careful inventory of what your days and weeks are like. Then see if you have enough room to add a foster dog into your busy schedule. Ask yourself questions like: Do I have time to get to really know the rescue dog, and to properly evaluate it? Can I take the afternoon (or a couple of days, if needed) off from work to get the dog spayed or neutered, and to follow up on post-surgery care? Is there time in my day for housetraining, basic obedience training, crate training, working through special problems, etc.? Will I have the time to meet and screen potential adopters?

- **Your experience.** You can learn a lot about dogs from books, but nothing beats experience when it comes to fostering a rescue. Each dog will be different, and it will bring with it a whole new set of concerns and situations. You may want to wait until you have more "dog experience" before you take on a foster dog. A good way to gain experience is to work closely with an established rescue person and with several rescues.

- **You.** It's easy for folks to grow weary of doing rescue because, quite simply, it's a lot of work! In addition, the emotional attachment between the rescuer and the dog can become quite strong. Only you can tell if you're up to the challenge of fostering dogs and, eventually, letting them go to their new homes. It's a good idea to talk with people who are already involved with rescue and get a good feel for what's involved. Be sure to ask a lot of questions — the more you understand what you're getting into, the better able you'll be to handle whatever comes your way!

### Rescue Pickup and Transport

Can't foster a dog but still want to help? If you have a vehicle that can safely hold a Basenji-sized dog crate, then maybe you can be involved with the transport of rescues. Folks in Basenji rescue sometimes have to rely on others to pick up dogs. If you think you'd like to be involved in this way, contact your local club or rescue organization and see if they could use a hand. Also, you'll want to see the Tailtip on the Basenji Underground Railroad (BUR) located after Section 4 in this handbook.

### Tattooing/Microchipping

If you're a dog tattooist, or if you do microchipping, check to see if your local Basenji rescue could use your services. Often, rescue groups will tattoo or microchip the dogs they place. Many times, folks who tattoo and microchip will donate their services to these groups.

## Fund Raising

Got some good ideas and need a place to put them to use? Then contact your local rescue group and see if they need help fund-raising. Medical and other expenses can sometimes put a strain on the budgets of the best-run rescue groups. Most clubs and organizations welcome new ideas for increasing revenue. You can volunteer your time and energies at any rescue fund-raising event — it's a lot of fun and you'll meet a lot of great people while working for an excellent cause!

## Dog Walking/Dog Sitting

Most dogs enjoy going for long walks! If you're willing to share your daily stroll or jog with a four-legged companion, locate a rescue person nearby. He or she would probably welcome your help in exercising their charges! Also, you may be able to help out the rescue folks when they're out of town or away at dog events by dog sitting any rescue that must stay behind.

## Donations

What better way to thank the rescue organization for your wonderful new companion than by donating dog food, supplies, or even copies of this book! Rescue groups often work on a limited (or non-existent) budget and rely heavily on donations from the placement of dogs and on fund-raising to help pay their bills. Anything you are willing to do to help them out is always greatly appreciated. As an added bonus, donations to organizations such as Basenji Rescue and Transport, Inc. (BRAT) may be tax deductible! (For more information on BRAT, see the Tailtip on the Basenji Underground Railroad (BUR) located after Section 4 in this handbook.)

# Section 4. Questions You May Be Asked and Questions You Should Ask

Interviewing someone interested in adopting a rescue is a common practice among rescue groups. Keep in mind that the rescue folks have the welfare of the rescue Basenji at heart, and the more they know about you, the better they'll be able to tell if they have a dog that is right for you. You should be prepared for the questions a rescue person will ask you, and the questions listed here will help you understand what will be asked, and why. We've listed some of the most commonly asked questions here, and we've provided explanations as to why the questions are being asked.

Honesty is always the best policy, and you should remember that no matter how desperately you may want a Basenji, what you really want is the right Basenji for your lifestyle. If you feel the rescue people aren't taking the time to find out about you, you should probably look elsewhere. Many of these questions are the same ones responsible breeders ask prospective puppy buyers. Responsible, reputable rescue folks care about where their rescues go, and by asking questions, they are trying to make sure your home is the right one for the rescue dog. While we can't possibly list every question you may be asked, the ones we've listed here are some of the most common ones.

Remember that at any point in the process of looking for a rescue you can back out if you feel unsure. If you don't feel that a dog is right for you, you won't be doing anyone a favor by taking it anyway. Try not to make your decision to adopt a dog simply because you feel sorry for it.

## Have you ever owned a dog before?

Whether this will be your first Basenji or your fifth, what the rescue person is looking for is whether or not you have "dog" experience. There is no right or wrong answer. Your answer will guide the rescue person and help him or her determine what additional information you may need, especially if a Basenji is your first dog.

## If you have owned a dog before, do you still have it? If not, what happened to it?

This question is important to the rescue person for many reasons. If you currently have a dog, then the rescue person needs to know ahead of time so that your dog and the rescue can be properly introduced. Perhaps your current dog won't get along with another dog in the house, or maybe there aren't any rescues available that are good with other dogs. If you don't have your dog any longer, tell the rescue person what happened to it, no matter if it ran away, was stolen, or had to be put to sleep for some reason.

### Have you ever owned a Basenji before?

Wonderful for you if you've lived with and loved a Basenji (or Basenjis). Don't be shy! Tell the rescue person all about the Basenji (or Basenjis) you've owned. This tells the rescue person that you have Basenji experience and already have a good working knowledge of the breed and its habits. Even if you've never owned a Basenji before, don't worry. Good owners are good owners, whether they love Basenjis or Boxers or Brittanys.

### If you have owned a Basenji before, do you still have it? If not, what happened to it?

As with the previous question, the rescue person needs to know about your experience with Basenjis. If you have another Basenji in the household, the rescue person will want to know all about it. Then, they will try to match you up with a rescue that will get along with your dog. Again, if you don't have your Basenji any longer, tell the rescue person what happened to it, no matter if it ran away, was stolen, or had to be put to sleep.

## Why are you interested in Basenjis?

People are interested in different breeds for different reasons. Sometimes they have a preconceived notion of what a particular breed is like, simply because they saw it in a movie or had a friend who had a particular dog. All breeds of dog are unique, and the Basenji is no exception. Be sure to tell the rescue person as best you can why you are interested in Basenjis. No answers are right or wrong — they simply serve to help the interviewer find out what your expectations are.

## What sorts of research have you done on Basenjis? What books have you read? Who have you talked to about Basenjis?

By answering this question you can show the rescue person you've done your homework. It is always beneficial to find potential adoptive homes where the people have taken the time to research and understand the breed. This also helps the rescue person find out what your expectations are, and it lets them see that you have a good understanding of the breed.

## Are there any other breeds that you are interested in?

If you are looking at Basenjis and considering other breeds of dogs as well, let the interviewer know. He or she may be able to tell you how Basenjis differ from other breeds. This will help you make your decision, and it will help the interviewer understand your needs and expectations as well. If you're only interested in Basenjis, that's fine too.

## What do you like about Basenjis?

Again, your answer here will tell the rescue person whether or not you have done your homework, and it will let him or her know what your expectations are about the breed and its characteristics.

## What don't you like about Basenjis?

Nobody likes every quality of every breed. Be prepared to tell the rescue person what you don't like, in addition to what you do like. They should be able to tell you if what you don't like is actually true. You may find that you had a preconceived notion about Basenjis that simply isn't true. Or maybe the breed characteristic you dislike is present in varying degrees, making one rescue dog more suitable for you than another. Your answer to this question may also help in the decision of whether or not to place a rescue with you. If you don't like the fact that Basenjis

can't be allowed to run loose, for example, then your rescue person may advise that you really don't want a Basenji at all, and instead you may want to consider some other breed.

## What would make you choose a Basenji over another breed of dog?

While this may seem like a repeat of a previous question, what the rescue person is looking for here is that you've looked at the positive as well as the negative aspects of the breed, and that in doing so you can explain why you would choose a Basenji. Is the Basenji the dog for you?

**What sort of dog are you looking for? Companion for yourself, for your kids, a running partner, etc.?**

Expectations and preconceived notions come into play here as well. You may be looking for a couch potato, an active dog, or a combination of the two. This is a question that only you can answer, and it's important enough that you should've already asked yourself this question. Answers that you give to this question make it easier for a rescue person to match up a dog with you and your lifestyle.

**Are you looking for a dog that you can allow off leash outdoors?**

*All* dogs should be properly leashed when not confined to their own yard. Some people are used to having dogs they can trust to stay close by when they are washing their car in the driveway. If you're looking for an off-leash dog, you don't want a Basenji. Granted, a few Basenji owners have had success in training their dogs to behave off-leash, but Basenjis, being sighthounds, are likely to chase anything that moves. In addition, most city and county ordinances don't allow dogs to roam freely. There are times when it will be safe for your Basenji to be off leash, but it's not a risk that most Basenji owners are willing to take.

**Do you have a preference — male or female dog?**

It's entirely up to you whether you prefer male dogs or female dogs. Keep in mind that a rescue is most likely going to be spayed or neutered before you are allowed to adopt it, so breeding and conformation showing are out of the question. It may be that the rescue person has a wonderful dog that's a perfect match for you, but it's a female instead of the male you preferred. Each dog is unique, and unless you're absolutely certain you will only consider one over the other, it shouldn't really matter if the dog is male or female — just as long as the dog is right for you.

**Do you live in a house, condo, or apartment? Do you rent or own? If you rent, does your landlord approve of dogs?**

Basenjis can live just as well in apartments and condos as they do in houses with big backyards. It's all a matter of how much exercise you can give the dog, and whether your landlord and neighbors accept it. If you own your home, great! If you live in a condo or an apartment, or if you rent your home, it's *absolutely necessary* to get permission before you even consider a dog.

Many people find that their landlords are agreeable to having a Basenji around, provided the dog is crate-trained and housebroken, and doesn't make itself a nuisance. If your landlord or condo association doesn't allow dogs and won't make an exception, don't expect a rescue person to allow you to adopt a dog. Most rescue groups will want to see a written O.K. before they adopt a dog out. Keep in mind that Basenjis, while barkless, are not mute and can be quite noisy at times. Also, the activity level of a Basenji running around in your apartment may not bode well with your apartment neighbors.

### Do you have a fenced-in yard? If not, how do you intend to keep your Basenji?

While many Basenji owners believe that the best place for a Basenji to be a Basenji is safe in it's own fenced-in yard, it doesn't mean you can't have a Basenji just because you don't have a fence. But you need to plan ahead as to how you'll exercise your dog, allow it to go "potty," etc. Many Basenji owners who can't or don't have fences have managed just fine, and this fact should not disqualify you from consideration for a rescue.

## Who will be the primary caregiver for the dog?

This is a very important question that you'll have to answer, especially if you have children and are getting the dog primarily for them. Your children may be the most wonderful children ever, but it isn't realistic to expect them to take full responsibility for feeding and caring for your Basenji. You should determine ahead of time who will feed and care for the dog. It's great if you can get your kids or partner to help. Unless you live alone and will be the primary caregiver of the dog, it's a good idea to discuss this with the other members of the household ahead of time so there are no surprises down the road.

## Does everyone in the family agree to getting a dog?

If the kids are all for it, and you are too, but your spouse just thinks it's a bad idea, maybe you should reconsider getting a dog. Marriages have been broken up and relationships strained from lesser things. Be sure everyone agrees that a Basenji is what the family wants before you bring it home. A rescue person may not allow you to adopt a dog if there's someone in the household who doesn't agree to it.

## Do you have children? If yes, what are their ages?

Some rescues are great with children, and some simply can't stand them. Realize that the background of the dog is what has made up its personality today. A dog that was constantly poked and prodded by someone's three-year old isn't a good candidate to live with yours. Some dogs aren't good around babies or small children, and they may have been given up to rescue for that reason. That's why everyone in the household should go to meet the rescue group and the rescue dogs.

## Do you have other pets? If yes, what kinds?

You should let the rescue person know If you have other pets. If you allow your pet ferret to roam the house when you're not home, or if your cats still have their claws, you may want to think carefully about bringing a dog into your home environment. Some rescues are fine with other pets, and some may not tolerate other pets at all. By letting your rescue person know what other creatures live in your home, he or she will be better able to find a dog that is right for you.

## How do you believe a dog should be disciplined?

Everyone has their own ideas on how to discipline a dog. If you caught your dog in the act of shredding some paper, or urinating on the rug, what would you do? Keep in mind that all dogs react differently to different people, and that while you may be able to discipline a dog fairly, your partner may have other ideas. The last thing a rescue person wants to do is to place a dog in a home where they believe the dog will be unfairly disciplined or abused.

Also, a dog that experienced abuse at the hands of its previous owner may require special treatment. The rescue person may need to decide if you can provide that type of special care and discipline that a formerly abused dog may need.

## Where do you plan on leaving the dog when you go on vacation or out of town on business?

How you answer this shows how much thought you've put into adding a new dog to your family. Do you plan on having your Basenji accompany you on vacations? Do you plan on boarding your Basenji when you have to go out of town on business? Planning ahead for such things shows that you're a responsible individual who has seriously considered the responsibility and commitment involved in adopting a dog.

## Is someone home all day? What are the hours that you/your family work/are in school?

Basenjis, like all other dogs, are social animals that need plenty of love, attention, and exercise. If someone is home all day, great! If you work, you'll need to think about how much time you spend at work, and how much time you'll be able to spend with your Basenji when you come home. Even though you may be tired from a long day, your Basenji will have been patiently awaiting your return, and he'll be happy to see you and ready to play. If you are always running your kids off to soccer practice and dance lessons after school, you may find that you just don't have time for a dog. Know what you can give, and what you can't.

Remember, the rescue person is looking for the best home for the rescue, and if you find that you simply don't have the time you thought you'd have, then you've saved yourself and the dog from an unhappy situation. On the other hand, if you find that you have plenty of time to spend with your new dog, both you and the dog will benefit from each other's company.

## Do you have an age preference as far as how young/ old of a dog you'd like to adopt?

Unless you feel very strongly about age, the age of the dog you adopt really shouldn't make a difference. Keep in mind that, barring any unforeseen accident or illness, your Basenji may live to be 15 or 16 years old. Even an eight-year-old Basenji still may have eight good long years ahead of it. Take into account the dog's age before you adopt it, but don't let age be the only deciding factor.

Realize that you're probably not going to find a cuddly, eight-week-old puppy in rescue. The vast majority of rescues are between two and seven years of age. As a rule, Basenjis age rather well, and they can remain active well into their teens.

**Are you involved with any breed clubs, showing, obedience work, therapy work, etc.? Do you have any dog-related hobbies or affiliations?**

If you're involved in dog-related activities, let the rescue person know. This will tell the rescue person how much experience you have with dogs and what kind of dog you might be looking for. If you aren't yet involved in these types of activities, the rescue person might be able to suggest some organizations or clubs of interest to you. You may find that your Basenji will open new and exciting doors for you, and you can make many new friends by joining a breed club or going to a training class. But even if these activities aren't for you, there are many other ways you and your Basenji can enjoy being together!

**Could you give us some personal references?**

Just like on a job application, the references you give should be people who know you well. Don't be surprised if you're asked for two or three references before you're allowed to adopt a rescue Basenji. It's just another way for the rescue folks to find out what you're all about, and to confirm what they've already decided about you.

**Do you understand the terms of the adoption and agree to them?**

Make sure you've had a chance to read *all* the material that the rescue people give you before you sign anything. You may have more questions. Most of the time the adoption agreement will specify that the dog will be spayed or neutered, and that you must return the dog to the rescue group if you no longer want it or if you're unable to care for it. See Section 5 of this handbook, "Adoption Applications and Rescue Adoption Contracts," for more information.

**We would like to make a house visit with the rescue. When would be a good time?**

Most rescue groups will want to make a visit to your home before they allow you to adopt a rescue. Let them know they are welcome to come, and set up an appointment to do so. If possible, schedule a time when most of your family will be home. The rescue people will probably want to bring the rescue dog with them when they come, just to see how the dog and your family interact in your home environment. When the rescue people are visiting, you may want to ask them to take a "tour" of your home. They may be able to suggest ways you can make your home Basenji-safe.

**Do you have any questions you'd like to ask us?**

Oh, yes, you do! The following pages have questions you should ask rescue people — and the answers you should expect to hear.

In addition to filling out an adoption application and being interviewed by someone (or several someones) from the rescue group, you should do a little interviewing of your own. The following questions are some of the most important ones you can ask about the dog you are thinking of adopting, and the answers you get will give you a good idea of how well the rescue group has its act together. The rescue group should welcome your questions and answer them as completely as they can. After all, the rescue group exists solely for the dogs it rescues, and its purpose is to help find new homes where the dogs will fit in well and spend the rest of their days. By asking these questions, you'll show them you're serious about adopting a Basenji, and that you're willing to do your homework to make sure the adoption will work out. Finding out the answers to these questions will give you confidence in the rescue group, and they'll help you better understand the Basenji you're thinking of adopting.

Beware of any rescue person or group that isn't open with their answers, doesn't want to answer questions, or is "offended" by the fact that you are asking questions. Remember, there are other fish in the sea, and if you're not confident that the rescue organization is doing what it can to see that dogs are matched up properly with new owners, then you don't want to deal with them at all. It's always better to be safe than sorry, and it's better to find out ahead of time and save heartbreak later.

## What is the background on the dog? Why did the previous owner give the dog up for rescue?

This question will help you establish the history of the dog. You may find out how many homes the dog has lived in, how it came to be in rescue, and why it was given up. If the dog was placed in a shelter, the rescuer may know why. If the dog was picked up as a loose stray, you need to know that, too. Whatever the reason the dog ended up in rescue, the rescuer should be able to tell you as much as he or she can about any dog available for rescue. By asking this question you're showing the rescuer that you're interested in the past history of the dog, and the answers you get here may help you determine whether or not any particular dog is right for you.

Don't assume that a dog will be unsuitable just because it has lived in many homes during a relatively short period of time. Even the sweetest of dogs can suffer from a string of misfortunes. Explanations like "They had a new baby and the dog wasn't getting any attention" or "They had to move to an apartment and couldn't take the dog along" are common. It's not unusual for the previous owner to unjustly blame the dog for its previous situation, so make sure you get all the facts when you talk to the rescue people. For example, a dog that is labeled as "unusually destructive" may not have been getting the attention it needed.

So, be sure to ask the rescue people about their experiences with the dog since it was taken into rescue. Many times you will find that a dog living in a new situation with the proper care and attention will exhibit much better behavior than it did previously.

Be very wary if you are told that the dog is aggressive, or if you find out that the dog has bitten someone. If the dog has been aggressive or has bitten, try to find out what provoked the incident, if you can. Once a dog has bitten, it is forever on "probation" according to the laws in many areas, and it may bite again in similar circumstances. This is something you want to find out up front. Most people don't want the responsibility of a known biter, and a reputable rescue group will not place dogs that are aggressive or known biters.

**What sorts of  health records do you have on the dog?**

Health records may have accompanied the rescue when it was turned in, either to the rescue group or to the shelter. If the dog was picked up as a loose stray, there probably aren't any health records on the dog except those that the rescue group may have. You need to be sure the rescue person has had the dog vet-checked and wormed, and that all shots are in order. If you decide to adopt the dog, ask for the health records. (The rescue group will probably keep photocopies of these records.) Be wary of anyone who tells you they haven't had the dog vet-checked, especially if the dog was picked up at a shelter.

**Does the dog have any medical problems?**

What you're looking for here is to find out if the dog has allergies, skin diseases, eye problems, hip and joint problems, etc. You generally want to get an overview of the dog's overall health. The rescuer should be very familiar with the dog and be able to tell you these things. The dog should be free of worms, fleas, and other parasites. Often there are dogs available for adoption that have certain hereditary diseases or allergies that are easily managed.

You should not necessarily be turned off by an adoption prospect simply because it may have special needs. However, if you're considering adopting a dog that has special needs, you'll want to be sure you have a full understanding of what care and costs will be involved in managing those needs.

**Do you have the dog's registration papers (AKC, CKC, etc.)?**

A rescue may or may not have registration papers. Because you are looking to adopt a pet, registration papers really aren't necessary because you won't be showing or breeding the rescue. But, papers can help define the origin of the dog, and can be helpful when researching pedigrees for health reasons. What you may find is that there are registration papers on the dog, but it's the rescue group's policy not to release the originals with the dog. Rather, once the dog is adopted, they send the papers back to the registration organization (the American Kennel Club, for example), letting them know that the dog has been rescued. In this way, the rescue group is assured that the dog will not be able to produce any litters that are registrable, thus helping prevent more rescues in the future. Upon adopting a dog, you may be given a copy of the papers for your own records if the originals are available.

## Has the dog been spayed or neutered?

Female dogs are spayed (surgically altered so they cannot reproduce) and male dogs are neutered (surgically altered so they cannot reproduce). If the dog you're interested in isn't already spayed or neutered, the rescue group will probably want to make sure the dog is spayed or neutered before it is adopted, or shortly after. In this way the rescue group insures that the dog is not able to produce any puppies and contribute to the general pet overpopulation problem.

Rescue groups may either include the cost of this in their adoption fee, or they may tell you it's an additional charge. Many people don't know that there are benefits to having a dog that is spayed or neutered. Your rescue person or veterinarian should be able to explain these benefits to you.

## How old is the dog?

The rescue group may know the age of the dog for sure, or they may be guessing. If they are guessing, find out how they arrived at the dog's estimated age. Sometimes a veterinarian can determine approximately how old it is, and some breeders can, too. Knowing the age of the dog helps you to better understand how it will adapt to a new home, and it gives you a rough guess of how many years the dog may have left to live. Don't be turned off by a dog simply because it's older or because its age is unknown. Older dogs that are rescued often are most appreciative of their new homes and bond closely with their new owners.

## Is the dog housetrained?

The answer you would like to hear is "yes," but don't be discouraged if the answer is "no." The rescue person should take the time to housetrain a rescue if it needs to learn, but there may be underlying reasons for the dog not to be. If the dog isn't housetrained, you should ask why and find out what the rescue person is doing to help train the dog. Often you may find unaltered (not neutered) male dogs that like to lift their legs inside the house. This practice may subside somewhat after a dog is neutered. Sometimes spayed females may exhibit "spay incontinence." This condition can often be managed with a daily medication.

## Is the dog crate trained?

Crate training is important. If the dog isn't crate trained, the rescue person should be working on this with the dog. See the Tailtip on crate training, after Section 6 of this handbook, for more information.

## What sort of obedience training has the dog had?

This will give you a good indication of what the dog knows and doesn't know and, perhaps, how much of a challenge the dog will be. However, just because a dog isn't an obedience champion, it doesn't mean it won't be an excellent companion for you. Basenjis are highly intelligent creatures, and they can be trained if you go about it with patience, fairness and a good sense of humor. Ask the rescue person if they can recommend an obedience training class that has experience with Basenjis.

## Is the dog good with children?

What you do with the answer to this question really depends on you. What are you looking for in the rescue? Do you want a dog that will play fine with your kids or with kids in your neighborhood? Maybe you don't have children, and the dog will rarely be in contact with them. The rescue person should be able to tell you how the dog acts with children of various ages. If you have children, make arrangements to observe the dog interacting with them. Do this several times so you are confident that your kids and the dog will be able to get along. See Section 7, "Children and Dogs: Knowing the Rules," for more information.

**Is the dog known to be destructive? Does it chew furniture, urinate on furniture, etc.?**

Sometimes it's easy to identify a destructive dog, and sometimes it's not. Some dogs are only destructive under certain circumstances. For example, destructive behavior may occur only when a dog is alone or stressed. Many Basenjis are destructive inside their crates, shredding bedding or toys, but they don't do any harm when outside. Others are destructive only when left alone for long periods or when they don't get enough attention. Each Basenji is unique, and, by finding out the answer to this question, you'll be prepared and won't have any surprises later on. The

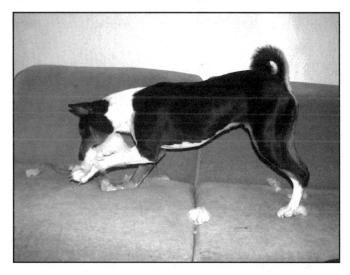

rescue person should know the dog well enough to give you a good behavioral profile. Another example of a destructive behavior is urinating in the house. The dog may not have been properly housetrained, or it may be an unaltered male marking his territory. Urinating in the house could also be an indication of a physical problem, so it's important to understand the reason for this behavior. The key to correcting any type of destructive behavior is understanding the cause, and then working toward a solution.

**What sort of follow up (visits, phone calls) can I expect from you if I adopt?**

The answer you get here really helps you to determine if you want to rescue a dog from this person/group or not. Reputable rescue organizations may insist on not only a home visit before they let you adopt a dog, but they will also follow up after the adoption with several phone calls to find out how the dog is doing. If they don't seem to care about what happens to the dog after it's placed, then you really should consider looking elsewhere.

**Is there a trial period during which I can return the dog if things don't work out?**

Many rescue organizations will allow you a trial period, usually a couple of weeks or so, to see if you and the dog are a good match. Within this time you should be able to get your money back and return the dog if things don't work out. Be aware, though, that careful consideration goes into the placement of rescues, and you shouldn't take the adoption responsibility lightly.

**Will you take the dog back if I can no longer care for it?**

Circumstances can arise in anyone's life that cause upheaval and change in a household, and unfortunately no one can predict if or when these events will take place. If you can no longer care for the dog, or if for some reason you are unable to keep it, the rescue contract should specifically state that the rescue group will take the dog back. This is one good way to tell if the rescue group is "on the up-and-up," and it shows that they take responsibility for the dogs they place.

**Why do you think I might be a good adoption candidate for this dog? (Or why not?)**

Honesty is always the best policy, and because the rescue group has the dog's best interests at heart, you shouldn't be disappointed if for some reason they decide that you aren't a match for any of the dogs they currently have available. Each dog is unique, and each adoption should be treated this way as well. The purpose of the interview process in rescue is to determine which is the best home for the rescued dog, and you should trust the rescuer's judgment. The rescuer should tell you whether or not you're a good candidate, and they should explain the reasons to you.

*The Secondhand Basenji Handbook*

After the interview is complete and all parties have had an opportunity to ask questions, relax! If the interview takes place at a location where rescues are housed, visit with the available dogs for a while. Try to get a feel for each dog's "personality," and see how the dogs respond to you.

Don't expect a final "yes" or "no" decision on the adoption right away. The rescuer may want to take some time to consider if you're a good match with any of the available rescues, or he or she may need to consult with other members of the rescue group before making a decision.

You'll need some time to think, too! Acquiring a pet is always a big responsibility and commitment, and you'll want to be certain you're making the right decision. Think about the rescuer and how he or she answered your questions. Ask to see an adoption contract, and make sure you understand the rescue group's policies and procedures. (See the next section, "Adoption Applications and Rescue Adoption Contracts" for information on applications and contracts.) Think about the rescues you met, and the breed in general, and consider whether it's a good match for your lifestyle. The adoption process can seem to move pretty slow sometimes, especially when you're excited about (maybe) welcoming a new pet into your heart and home. The rescuer may want to meet with you one or two more times, at your home or elsewhere, before a decision is made and the adoption process is completed. Make sure you know what's next each step of the way. Try to be objective — don't let that beautiful dog you met cloud your thinking!

## Tailtip – Rescuers Across the Miles: The Basenji Underground Railroad

If you're looking for a rescued Basenji in the United States or Canada, chances are pretty good that someone will recommend you contact the BUR or the BRAT.

You may wonder what exactly they're talking about, because "burrr" describes a sound Basenjis sometimes make when happy, and a "brat" is usually someone who can get on your nerves! But the BUR and BRAT we're speaking of are neither of these two things — in fact, they represent what is perhaps the most organized group of Basenji folks around when it comes to rescue and adoption!

Developed out of a need to help rescued Basenjis across the United States and Canada, Basenji Rescue and Transport, Inc. (BRAT) and the Basenji Underground Railroad (BUR) boast over 200 members (to date) working hard to help Basenjis in need find new homes.

Although rescue groups usually try to place dogs locally, sometimes they need to transport dogs to new homes located outside of the area in which the dog was rescued. In the past, rescue folks didn't (or simply couldn't) place dogs outside of their own locale for various reasons — transportation was often too time-consuming or expensive, airlines wouldn't ship dogs in certain types of weather, and the rescuers had no good way of screening potential out-of-town adopters, etc.

But "underground railroads" have overcome those obstacles. In the doggy world, an underground railroad is a network of volunteers who help transport rescued dogs to new homes. Utilizing the Internet, these folks set up a relay to transport dogs across the country to new homes. Each person in the relay usually drives the dog 100 to 200 miles (160 to 320 km) of the trip toward its new home. Because all underground railroad activities are required to remain within the law (including laws requiring rabies vaccinations), illegal means are *not* advocated to save dogs that might be perceived as being in peril.

**How do the BUR and BRAT work?**

BRAT members monitor local animal shelters, humane societies, classified ads, and the Internet to locate Basenjis in need. Many of these folks are also Basenji Club of America rescue coordinators, so they learn of potential rescues through telephone calls from shelters or from owners who have decided to give up their dogs. Sometimes owners who are having difficulties with their Basenjis contact BRAT for help placing the dogs, and the BRAT representatives are able to offer ideas and/or resources to help the owners resolve easily remedied problems and avoid placement.

When a BRAT member learns of a Basenji in need of rescue in his or her area, the member contacts the person (or shelter) who has the dog and tries to get ownership of the animal transferred to BRAT. Each dog is evaluated as soon as it's in BRAT's possession, then all of the dog's information (and sometimes its photo) is sent to the BRAT web site. The web site has directories of Basenjis and Basenji mixes that are available for adoption, and BRAT updates the information as promptly as possible. (See "Basenjis on the Internet" in Appendix A of this handbook for the BRAT web site address.)

There's also a BRAT adoption application form on the web site that interested people can fill out. Once you submit the form, you'll have access to e-mail notices of rescue Basenjis as soon as they become known to BRAT — and before they are actually listed on the web site.

If you see a dog you're interested in, you can contact the designated BRAT coordinator for that dog. The coordinator will review your application, and the coordinator will communicate with you regarding your expectations and what he or she knows about the Basenji. The coordinator is responsible for evaluating all possible options for the Basenji and selecting the very best match. Be prepared to ask and answer lots of questions! Adoption is a tremendous commitment, and BRAT coordinators put a great deal into each and every placement. Reference checks and a home visit are quite common.

Once a new home is selected, the adoptive family and the coordinator may begin planning to transport the dog if the placement is not local. There are times when air transport or a short drive by the adoptive family are not options, and BUR resources make all the difference in getting the Basenji "home." While not everyone can foster or place a rescued Basenji, many people find the time to help the BUR. Volunteers drive the dog a few hours each, making it possible for the rescue to be delivered to its new home.

So, if you're considering a rescued Basenji, or if you'd like to help BRAT or the BUR by volunteering or making a financial donation (your donation to BRAT may be tax deductible!), you can learn more about these organizations by visiting their web sites. See "Basenjis on the Internet" in Appendix A of this handbook for the web site addresses.

# Section 5. Adoption Applications and Rescue Adoption Contracts

Adoption applications are used by rescue groups to screen people interested in adopting a rescue. By filling out an adoption application, the rescue group learns about you and your expectations, and they are better able to decide if you'll be a good match for a Basenji they're trying to place. When you receive an application, fill it out as completely as you possibly can. Don't worry that you'll be turned down just because you've never owned a dog before, your yard isn't fenced in, or you have six children. It's the job of the rescue group to find out about you and determine if they have a dog that is suitable for your specific situation.

## Rescue Adoption Application Example

The following is an example of an adoption application. Not all adoption applications you see will be the same — some may ask for even more information, and others may ask only a few questions. This example is from the Basenji Rescue and Transport, Inc. web site. (See "Basenjis on the Internet" in Appendix A of this handbook for the web site address.)

## The Secondhand Basenji Handbook

Completing this form is a prerequisite to adopting a Basenji through Basenji Rescue and Transport, Inc. The information you provide helps our coordinators match you and your family with just the right dog (hence, the length of the form).

Answer the form as completely as you can. Any information you can not or do not want to supply, leave blank. Your responses will only be used in rescue-related activities but will be posted to a private Web site and will be read by a network of BRAT rescue workers and coordinators. Your information may also be transmitted via e-mail to the same.

If you are serious about adopting a rescue and you express interest in a particular dog expect interviews, reference checks and possibly a home-visit from a BRAT coordinator before the adoption is finalized.

If you don't know much about Basenjis we encourage you to read some of our Reality Stories. These stories may enlighten you to the quirks of the breed. Or check our links for other Basenji rescue-related and general-information sites.

Finally, please note that either BRAT or any local club placing the Basenji may charge an adoption fee of up to $150.00 to cover direct and indirect expenses incurred in their rescue program.

Thank you for your interest in adopting a rescue and thank you for using the BRAT site!

## Personal Information About You and Your Family:

Name:               Address:                    City / State / Zip:

Work Phone:       Best time to call:        Home Phone:                Best time to call:

Accept collect calls?       Yes       No

E-mail address (required):

Please enter a valid e-mail address or type the word none. Click here to view rules for a valid e-mail address.

How often do you read your e-mail?

Age:          Occupation:

Are you married?        Yes       No                How many children?          Age:

Are you expecting a child or planning a family?        YesNo

Do children regularly visit your home?              Yes       No

List all other dogs in the household (include breed, age and sex):

How long have you owned the dog(s)?

How many cats?          Sex:                        Have other critters?       Yes       No

Vet's Name:               Vet's Address:                Vet's City / State / Zip:                          Vet's Phone:

We live in a:          House                      Apartment/Condo

We:        Own        Rent                  Landlord allows dogs?  Yes        No        Not sure

Our neighborhood is:     Urban        Suburban               Rural

We have a secure yard?      Yes         No                    Describe your fence (height and type):

Tell us anything else about your family you'd like to:

Have you owned a Basenji?    Yes       No

Have you read any books about Basenjis?

What do you know about them?

Have you met a Basenji?       Yes        No

Have you spoken to a Basenji owner?     Yes            No

Would you like to visit a Basenji or have one visit you?      Yes       No

Who referred you to BRAT?

**Information about the dog you want:**

Gender:     Male     Female     Either

Color:     Red     Black     Tri     Brindle     Any color

Age:

Would you consider a Basenji mix?     Yes     No

Generally speaking, what kind of temperament are you looking for in a dog?

What qualities appeal to you about the Basenji?

Do you support crating?     Yes     No

Will you spay/neuter?     Yes     No     If no, why not?

Where will the Basenji stay when it's alone?          Where will the dog sleep?

Please add any other expectations or concerns you have:

Would you like more information about Basenjis?

## Rescue Adoption Contract Example

Adoption contracts are used by rescue groups to inform you of their rules and policies. Contracts not only protect the rescue group and the rescue dog, but also serve to protect you as well. Rescue contracts spell out what the rescue group expects you to do with the dog, as well as what they expect you not to do.

The contract may also include a return policy clause and a statement that you agree to never sell or give the dog away without first informing the rescue group. Most rescue groups will take dogs back, and the contract should indicate this if it is their policy. The contract should also state the price that you will pay for the dog, as well as require you to have the dog spayed or neutered if it hasn't already been done.

*Before you sign any contract with any rescue group, make sure that you understand everything written on it, and don't be afraid to ask questions.*

The following is an example of an adoption contract. This example is from the Basenji Rescue and Transport web site. (See "Basenjis on the Internet" in Appendix A of this handbook for the web site address.) This contract is for information only and is to be used exclusively by authorized BRAT coordinators.

### Basenji Rescue And Transport, Inc. Adoption and Transfer Contract

Basenji Name:                                                  Age:

I.D. Type/No.:

Color: ( ) Red/White ( ) Black/White ( ) Tri-Color ( ) Brindle

Sex: ( ) Male ( ) Female

Basenji Rescue And Transport, Inc., a Texas non-profit corporation (BRAT), has established this Contract to detail the specific requirements to which the Adopter/Transferor must comply as a condition of the Adoption/Transfer of the pet Basenji whose name and description appear above.

I. ADOPTION

I agree to comply with the following requirements as part of the adoption process of the above named pet Basenji, and fully understand that failure to do so will result in this Basenji being returned to BRAT.

I also understand and agree that BRAT or its agent may visit my home upon reasonable notice or make inquiry about said animal at any time and, if BRAT is not satisfied that the conditions of this Contract have been complied with, I agree to return the Basenji to BRAT without reimbursement or recourse. Moreover, should BRAT need to file legal action to reclaim the Basenji, I agree to pay all reasonable legal fees and expenses incurred by BRAT.

Upon execution of this Contract, I will become the legal owner of the pet Basenji and am responsible for the dog and its care. I have had the opportunity to have the Basenji checked by a Veterinarian of my choice before signing this Contract and I acknowledge that BRAT has made no warranties or guarantees of the dog's health. Furthermore, I acknowledge that BRAT has advised me of the following known defects and behavior or training problems of the Basenji:

A. I agree to supply and bring a collar, lead and pet carrier (crate) when picking up my pet Basenji.

B. I agree to reimburse BRAT, at the time of adoption, an adoption fee of $____ for coverage of any and all direct and indirect expenses incurred and paid by the club for the medical care, placement and well-being of my pet Basenji.

C. If I have not already done so, I agree to take my pet Basenji to a Veterinarian within three (3) days after adoption for a complete checkup; to purchase a city license according to my city ordinances (rabies certificate must be presented); to follow the animal ordinances of my city; and to attach a pet identification tag and/or veterinary tag to my pet Basenji's collar, which must be worn at all times when the Basenji is outside the home.

D. If my pet Basenji is not already spayed/neutered, I agree to have this done no later than twenty days after adoption (copy of veterinary charges sent to BRAT) or relinquish my right of ownership to BRAT. If the Basenji is under the age of six months, I agree that the dog will be spayed/neutered once the dog is six months old and I am providing a deposit of $100.00 to BRAT which will be refunded upon adequate proof of spay/neuter.

E. I agree to provide for my pet Basenji in a humane and responsible manner with adequate food, care and veterinary services, and agree that said animal shall not be used for medical or any other experimental purpose. For purposes of this Contract, humane and responsible care includes, but is not limited to, the following:

1. Provide Veterinary checkups annually;

2. Keep Immunizations current, according to AVMA guidelines;

3. Administer heartworm preventatives according to a schedule provided by your veterinarian.;

4. Provide adequate exercise for the Basenji and/or provide facility defined as a fenced area or kennel run. I specifically agree that the animal will not be kept on a chain and will have a heated space for sleeping.

5. Maintain the Basenji as a house pet and not use my Basenji for breeding purposes.

F. I agree to indemnify and hold BRAT harmless from any responsibility related to behavior deviations, illness or property damage occurring after adoption of my pet Basenji.

G. I agree not to sell, trade or give away my pet Basenji. If, at any time, I can no longer care for or keep my pet, I agree to return said animal to BRAT for no consideration.

I certify that all representations contained herein are true and correct and that I have read, understand and agree to the stipulations contained in this Contract.

Signed by Adopter:                          on this day of:

Printed Name:

Address:                          City:                          State:                          Zip Code:

Phone Numbers: (H) (     )                          (W) (     )

Agent's Name(s):                          Phone Number: (     )

BASENJI RESCUE AND TRANSPORT, INC.

By:

Printed Name:

Its:

## Tailtip – "Golden Opportunity" Dogs: Breeders Finding Homes for Basenjis

Basenjis in search of new homes aren't necessarily all considered to be rescues. In fact, many breeders routinely place Basenjis (who aren't puppies) with new families. These dogs, sometimes referred to as "Golden Opportunity" dogs, can make wonderful companions

Golden Opportunity dogs may be dogs the breeder kept that never matured into show-quality animals, show dogs who never quite made it in the show circle, or even retired show champions. They may be dogs the breeder sold and then later agreed to take back for some reason. Whatever the circumstance, if you're looking for a dog who has a known background, is mature and has quite possibly had a bit of training, you may want to consider one of these Golden Opportunity dogs.

The best way to locate a Golden Opportunity dog is to get in touch with your local Basenji club. You can also talk to Basenji folks at dog shows, fun matches, or educational events. It wouldn't hurt to check with your local Basenji rescue folks, either. Often, rescue groups and breeders work together to help each other locate and screen homes for Basenjis in need.

As with any other adoption, you'll want to ask lots of questions and follow the advice in this handbook when choosing your Golden Opportunity dog. Find out why the breeder is placing the dog, what the background and medical history of the dog is, and so on. One great advantage to considering a Golden Opportunity dog is that the dog's background, training, and socialization are usually well known by the person placing the dog.

Also, just like with an adoption, you should expect to be interviewed by the breeder — a process that may be much like the screening process used to help find homes for rescues. Most likely, there will be some sort of contract the breeder will ask you to sign, and you may be required to spay or neuter the dog, if it hasn't already been done. In addition, you may also get the registration papers and pedigree of your new dog.

As with rescues, folks placing Golden Opportunity dogs want to be sure that you are the best home for the dog, and that the dog is the best one for you. And, the breeder will probably want to keep in touch with you and hear how your new companion is doing from time to time. Breeders usually make themselves available throughout the dog's lifetime to answer any questions and address any concerns you may have.

So, if you think a Basenji is right for you, but you aren't sure about adopting a rescue, check into the Golden Opportunity dogs that may be in your area. Who knows? You might find the perfect new member for your family!

# *NOTES*

# Section 6.  The Shelter Dog

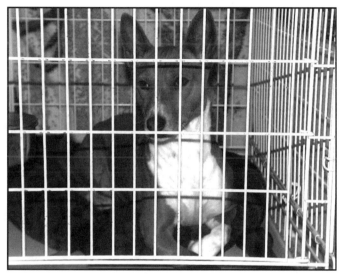

Adopting a shelter dog can be just as rewarding as adopting from a rescue organization. After all, rescue groups often get the dogs they rescue from animal shelters and humane societies!

There are several books on the market today that address the pros and cons of adopting from a shelter. To help make your shelter adoption a successful one, we suggest you refer to those publications for a thorough explanation of what to look for and what to avoid.

We can't possibly cover every topic relating to shelter animals in this handbook, but this section has some information you'll want to keep in mind when considering a dog that's being held by a shelter or humane society. We've compiled a list of questions you may want to ask the shelter or humane society personnel, and we've included some common questions people have about shelter dogs — and the answers.

# Questions you may want to ask:

### Q: Why is the dog in this shelter?

**A:** You'll want to find out as much about the dog as you can, and the first thing you'll want to learn is why the dog is there in the first place. Was it picked up as a stray? Did its previous owner give it up? Sometimes the shelter personnel will be able to tell you a lot about a particular dog. But sometimes they can't, especially if it's a busy facility. Try to learn as much about the dog's situation as you can, and keep a look out for clues to the dog's health status, personality, behavior with children and other pets, energy level, and any other qualities that may be important to you. This will help you decide if the dog is one you'd like to take home.

### Q: Has the dog ever bitten anyone?

**A**: If the answer to this question is "yes," the shelter may not even consider the dog to be adoptable. Keep in mind that people who turn their pets over to shelters aren't always up front as to their real reasons for doing so, and the shelter can only assume that what they've been told is true. For the safety of yourself and others, any dog that's a biter isn't one you should consider adopting.

**Q: Is the dog aggressive?**

**A:** Being in a shelter situation is a stressful thing for any dog, and the dog's true nature may not be easily determined in that environment. Often, dog-aggressive animals will show their tendencies, as will people-aggressive animals. If the dog growls or snaps at you, you may not want to adopt it, especially if you have children. As with a biter, the shelter may not even consider an aggressive dog adoptable.

**Q: How long has the dog been in the shelter? When will the dog be available for adoption?**

**A:** Some shelters have rules which require them to hold onto an animal for a specified period of time. This gives the shelter personnel time to assess the dog's health and well-being, and it gives owners time to find their lost or stray animals. There's a certain amount of liability involved here, especially when it comes to lost or stray dogs, so a shelter is going to stick to its rules. Also, shelter personnel may need time to determine the temperament of the animal and perform an evaluation to see if it is indeed adoptable.

**Q: Are there any records available on the dog?**

**A:** This may seem like a strange question, especially since we're talking about an animal that's a stray or that's been given up by its owner. However, some owners who give up their pets also provide the shelter with vaccination and other veterinary records, so the shelter or the new owner will have a history on the animal. Of course, you'll not find any records on a dog that's been picked up as a stray, but if you're looking at an animal that's been given up, there's a good chance you'll be able to acquire some sort of documentation on it.

**Q: What's the shelter's policy on spaying or neutering?**

**A:** As with most rescue organizations, shelters and humane societies most likely will require that a dog is spayed or neutered before it leaves to go home with you. Or, they may require you to sign a form by which you promise to return with the animal to have it spayed or neutered, or that you'll provide them with some sort of proof that spaying or neutering has been done.

**Q: What does it cost to adopt a dog?**

**A:** Costs of adoption will vary from shelter to shelter. You shouldn't have to pay any more for a purebred dog than you would for any other dog at the shelter, but you'll probably have to cover the costs relating to spaying or neutering. Some shelters will also charge you for the vaccinations that they've given the animal, and many will require you to pay for a dog license at the time of adoption.

## Common questions people have:

**Q:  The shelter personnel told me that the dog I'm considering adopting is on "death row."   I'm not yet sure I want to adopt it, though.  What should I do?**

**A:** Never feel forced into making a decision to adopt based strictly on the fact that the animal is scheduled to be put to sleep. If you're truly interested in adopting but need more time to decide, it's certainly okay to ask the shelter people to delay euthanizing the dog for a day or so. Most likely, they'd much rather adopt the dog out than destroy it, unless the dog is dangerous or has an unstable temperament. Or, you can let a local rescue organization or Basenji Rescue and Transport, Inc. know about the dog. (See "Basenjis on the Internet" in Appendix A of this handbook for the BRAT web site address.) A rescue person may be able to take the dog, giving you more time to decide if the dog is right for you. Don't make the mistake of adopting a dog purely out of sympathy — you may not like what you end up with, and you may end up facing the heartbreaking decision of having to return it to the shelter yourself.

**Q: I'm afraid the Basenji I'm adopting from the shelter will have fleas or some disease. What precautions can I take?**

**A:** No reputable shelter will allow the adoption of an animal known to be seriously ill or diseased. However, it's always a good idea to plan a veterinarian visit with your new dog as soon as possible. You'll want your vet to give the dog a thorough examination, checking for heartworm and intestinal parasites, in addition to checking for fleas. You should also have your vet check for kennel cough and other doggy ailments, especially if you have other animals at home. Although it can be expensive, you should consider having complete blood work done to check the functioning of the dog's vital organs and to detect diseases that are not yet showing symptoms.

**Q: I'm not interested in getting a Basenji right now, but I saw one in an animal shelter. Should I contact a Basenji rescue organization and let them know? What should I do?**

**A:** If you've seen a Basenji in the shelter, the information would certainly be welcomed by your local rescue organization or by a national group such as Basenji Rescue and Transport, Inc. (See "Basenjis on the Internet" in Appendix A of this handbook for the BRAT web site address.) Often, shelters and rescue groups work together, and the rescue group may already be aware that the dog is there. But this could be a life or death situation for the Basenji, so by all means inform a rescue group of the dog you've seen!

## *Tailtip – Crate Training Yourself and Your Basenji*

I recently overheard a co-worker describing in great detail how his two young puppies had knocked over the Christmas tree while he and his wife were away at work. He remarked how surprised he'd been to discover that, even though many of the glass ornaments had been broken, the dogs were unharmed. They had even chewed through some of the light strings that were on the tree! Luckily his dogs were fine, and he was able to clean up the mess before his wife came home. How terrible it would've been if the dogs had been injured or even worse, if they had started a fire by chewing on the light strings! Funny how it took this incident before this fellow decided that he was going to buy crates for his dogs and crate train them. You're lucky you don't have to find out the hard way — we hope you're going to start your new Basenji off right with his own crate.

Now, for many people, the word "crate" brings to mind a small box or perhaps a small wire cage.

Some folks may even envision thick metal bars like at a zoo. Instead of what your impression of a crate might be, let's consider for a moment what your Basenji thinks of it.

*"I like my crate. It's a place that's all my own. When my people can't watch me, they put me in my crate so I'll be safe. There's a lot of things to get into here at home, and there are things that, if I play with them, could hurt me or could break. I know that I'm safe in my crate. I think of my crate as my den, my safe haven, and my "dinnertime" spot. My people feed me in here, which is really nice because the other dog in my house can't eat my food."*

*"It's also nice to have a crate because I like to take a little nap after I eat, and since I'm already in my crate, I can just curl right up and go to sleep! My crate is in the quiet part of the house, so when noisy company comes over and I am tired, I can take a break and not be bothered by the people. When no one's home, I usually sleep most of the time anyway, so being in my crate is just fine with me. (I get plenty of exercise when my people come home!) I always have some of my favorite chew toys in my crate to keep me occupied while I'm there, too."*

Now, here's a person's view of the dog crate:

*"It's nice that my Basenji is crate trained. That way, when I can't watch him, I know he's safe. He can't get into things and chew on things he's not supposed to. It's nice to know that when company comes over, I can put him in his crate and he'll be able to enjoy some quiet time away from all the commotion. The crate is also where I feed my Basenji, and I can make sure he's eating well. I can tell right away if he's not feeling well, because he always eats all his dinner — when he doesn't, I know something might be wrong. I give my Basenji all sorts of safe chew toys and treats in his crate, and he's learned that when I say "naptime" or "dinnertime" or "bedtime," it's time for him to go into his crate. The best part about the crate is that I know my dog is safe when I go to work, and I know when I come home there won't be a terrible mess to clean up! Also, when I take my dog to the vet and he has to stay there awhile, or when I go away on a trip and can't take him with me, he's already used to being in his crate and doesn't mind."*

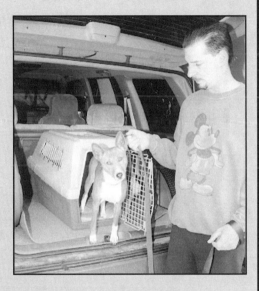

Life is so much easier (and safer) when you and your Basenji are crate trained!

# *NOTES*

# Section 7. Children and Dogs: Knowing the Rules

Maybe when you were a child you loved dogs — loved them so much that when you walked home from school you took the route that would give you the most encounters with those friendly, furry creatures who looked forward to your visits every day. On the other hand, maybe as a child you were terrified of dogs and would plan the route home that gave you the fewest encounters with the barking, slobbering monsters who seemed to see each new day as a chance to take a bite out of you.

Most of us have some very fond childhood memories of dogs, but we've also had our share of frights as well. Perhaps some of the most important lessons we can teach our children involve their behavior and safety around dogs.

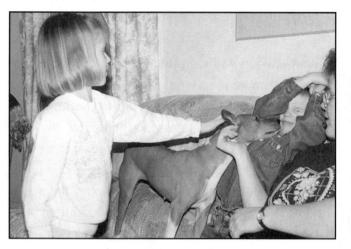

First and foremost, children should be taught at a very early age to never approach a dog they don't know. Children can be very trusting, especially when it comes to furry creatures. They need to understand that not every dog they meet is friendly. There's nothing that terrifies an apprehensive dog, or puts an aggressive dog on the offensive, more than a child screaming and running towards it at full speed, arms opened wide. Teach your children to avoid contact with loose or stray dogs, and if they meet someone walking a dog, teach your children to always ask permission before petting a dog. You never know, for example, when a dog you meet may have a special need, such as a partially blind dog that can only see what's on its right side and may be frightened by someone approaching from the left.

Second, children need to learn how to properly approach a dog, once they've been given permission to do so. Dogs, especially dominant or aggressive ones, are often challenged by someone who makes direct eye contact when approaching. Advise your children not to stare directly into a dog's eyes when they approach it. Have them offer their hand (closed into a fist or "paw" shape) and allow the dog to sniff them.

When petting a dog, teach your child not to go straight for the top of the dog's head. Instead, have them come up gently from under the chin and work their way around to the top of the dog's head. This way, the dog won't mistake an eager child's hand for a threatening "hitting" gesture. Instruct your children to be very gentle when they pet dogs — don't let them hug a dog tightly, poke, pull on the tail or ears, or do anything that could hurt the dog.

General behavior around dogs is also important. Some dogs can be "turned on" to a predator-prey mode if there are children running and screaming. Dogs can also be over-eager in their exuberance to play with children, and if they are too excited by the noise and activity, they may chase, nip, and knock the children over.

No matter how perfect your child may be, it's unreasonable to expect them to take full responsibility for the care of the family dog. Instead, you may want to assign specific tasks that match the age and maturity of the child. For instance, your twelve-year old may be an excellent candidate to take the dog out on daily walks; your six-year old isn't.

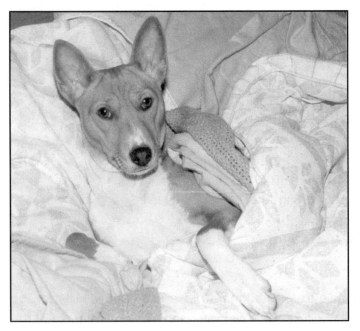

Another important thing for children to understand is that, just like them, dogs get tired and need quiet time. Your dog's crate should be off-limits to your children, and they need to learn to respect the dog's privacy during quiet time. Don't let your children tease or taunt a dog that is tied out or crated — most dogs are more likely to be aggressive when they feel cornered or confined. Teach your children that the phrase "let sleeping dogs lie" is a good rule to remember. Explain to them that, just as they wouldn't like being woken up at night by someone screaming at them or poking and picking them up, the same is true for the dog. Sleeping dogs — even the most trusted, laid back family dogs — are likely to bite out of fear when startled out of a sound sleep.

Taking the time to teach your children how to behave properly around dogs will help make each dog encounter they have a much safer and happier one.

Some other tips to keep in mind:

- Feed your dog in its crate, and don't allow children to bother it while it's eating. Also, when your dog is chewing on a treat or a toy, advise your children not to try to take the item away from the dog. If something needs to be taken away, they should ask an adult to do it.

- Teach your children to be careful about opening and closing doors. This will help prevent your dog from accidently "escaping." Make sure your dog wears identification and has a tattoo or a microchip implant in case he accidently gets loose.

- Be careful about what your children feed the dog. Sneaking the dog a chicken leg or a bone from dinner could cause an upset stomach, or the dog may choke on the bones. Warn your children not to feed the dog chocolate, other types of candy or anything other than dog food.

- Make sure your children pick up after themselves. This way, your dog won't be tempted to make a snack out of a favorite toy or a new pair of shoes.

- Never leave children unattended around dogs. Always supervise your dog around children — and your children around the dog — especially with guests or children your dog doesn't see frequently. Supervising play time with children and dogs will help avoid accidental injury to the dog and to the children.

- Babies don't know their own strength. Never leave a baby unattended with a dog, and never allow a baby to crawl on, grab, or poke at a dog. Also, avoid letting your dog lick the baby, and don't let the baby take toys away from the dog. Keep the dog toys and baby toys separate.

- Don't be too quick to blame the dog if he nips at or bites your child. Many dog bites are unknowingly provoked. Usually, the child doesn't realize that his or her behavior provoked the dog; so try to find out exactly what happened, and take appropriate steps to prevent it from happening again. If you discover the bite was unprovoked, or if you feel that your dog is becoming a threat to children, seek professional help immediately.

- Teach your children to respect the dog as a thinking, feeling creature. Set a good example for your children, and don't tolerate any sort of abuse aimed toward the dog.

- Children should be involved in the training of the dog. If you are taking your dog to obedience class, let your children come along. That way, while your dog is learning new commands, your children will also be learning them, so that everyone in the household can give the dog commands consistently. If everyone uses the same commands, it's much easier for the dog to understand what is being asked.

- Allow your dog to become an integral part of your family. Include him on family outings and walks, and in cozy evenings with the family in front of the television. Dogs are pack animals, and they will enjoy the company your family provides.

- Do your dog a favor and give him some quiet time if you're having a lot of company over all at one time, as you would for a birthday party. Sometimes children don't understand that the loud noise and popping balloons can be frightening for a dog. Also, the "fallout" from the party food isn't healthy for your pet.

- Your dog should have a crate where he sleeps, but it's okay to bend the rules once in a while and allow him to sleep with your child occasionally, provided your dog understands the rules of the bed. If your dog is possessive of a child's bed, growls when you approach him on the bed, or won't get off when you tell him to, you're much better off if he's not allowed up there at all.

## Tailtip – The Rumble of Thunder

The rumble of thunder in a dark gray sky may simply signal to you that a summer storm is approaching, but to your Basenji, it may be a terrifying sound. If your Basenji is afraid of thunderstorms, there are ways you can help him overcome his fear.

At the first rumble of thunder, try getting very excited with your Basenji. Tell him "Oh boy, THUNDER!" in a happy voice, and then while he's excited, tell him "Let's go get a COOKIE!" If you do this consistently, it may help your Basenji relax during storms. This conditioning works because your Basenji will associate the sound of thunder with treats, and he may eventually end up looking forward to storms!

Another good way to create a diversion is to have your Basenji run through his obedience commands during a storm. This helps your Basenji focus on you instead of the thunder outside, and this can help calm him. Also, try enticing your Basenji into playtime to help get his mind off the storm.

You may want to place your Basenji in his crate during thunderstorms. The crate is your Basenji's "safe haven," and he may actually feel safer and calmer in his crate than anywhere else when a storm is raging. Don't close the door to your Basenji's crate during a storm, so that he can move in and out of the crate freely. Don't force him to go in the crate if he doesn't want to, and don't make him feel trapped by locking him in.

Some dogs may prefer to hide under a bed or other furniture during storms, and that's fine if they seem to be calmer and more comfortable there. Don't make the mistake of dragging your dog out from his hiding place to face the storm the minute he runs and hides. If he wants to hide, let him. Forcing him to come out when he doesn't want to can actually make him become more fearful.

Some owners report that playing a recording of storm sounds helps to desensitize their Basenjis, so when storms really do take place, their Basenji is used to the familiar noise. If you want to try this method, begin by playing the recording at a very low level, so you can barely hear it. Play it over and over again, gradually increasing the volume as your Basenji becomes used to it. If he seems to be afraid, turn the sound down a little and distract him with treats, obedience commands, or try to entice him to play. It's a slow and gradual process, but after a few weeks, your Basenji should be much more relaxed when he hears the sound of thunder.

# *NOTES*

# Section 8. Planning and Preparing for the New Arrival

Congratulations! You're about to adopt a Basenji! If you plan ahead, you'll be able to welcome your new companion without wondering if you've forgotten something. Preparing and planning ahead makes the transition from rescue home to your home as stress-free as possible for your new Basenji and for you. Remember that the rescue probably has been through a lot of changes in the last few weeks or months, so you should do all you can to make your new dog's final adjustments to your home go smoothly. Do the work ahead of time and you'll be able to spend lots of time enjoying your new Basenji.

The first step in planning is to talk to the rescue person about the timing of your new arrival. The rescue people may want to keep the rescue for a few more weeks. They may want to monitor the dog's health or behavior, or they may need to spay or neuter the dog and allow some time for recovery. Be patient! Don't try to rush the adoption process at this point just because you can't wait to bring your new rescue home! Find out when the rescue person thinks your new Basenji will be ready for its new life with you. Then think about the events that will be taking place in your life or family at that time. Maybe you've planned a vacation, or maybe a holiday coming up means you'll be entertaining a house full of guests.

Dogs can adapt to almost any situation; but they need routine, especially when they're just getting used to a new home. Plan your arrival to coincide with a fairly stable, "normal" period in your family life.

One of the easiest ways to prepare for your new arrival is to do all of your shopping in advance. Find out from the rescue person what items they'll be providing with the dog. Some rescue groups include such basics as a leash, collar, and a toy or two with a rescue. Often you'll get a supply of whatever dog food the rescue person has been feeding your new Basenji. Whether they intend to provide you with dog food or not, find out what brands of food, treats, and vitamins the dog has been eating and buy at least a small amount of each. Also, find out when the rescue person has been feeding the dog during the day or evening. You can always change brands and feeding times later, but for now, plan on maintaining the diet and schedule the rescue Basenji is used to.

You'll also want to get the name, phone number, and location of the veterinarian the rescue group has been using. If it's convenient for you, you may want to continue seeing that particular veterinarian. If the current veterinarian isn't convenient for you, the rescue person may be able to suggest other veterinarians.

Write the veterinarian information on a card and post it in an easy to remember location, in case you ever need to find it quickly.

Remember that most rescue group budgets are usually tight. You can't expect to get a crate and all the other necessary dog supplies when you adopt. Especially if this is your first dog, you should expect to do some shopping in order to have all the necessary items on hand when your rescue comes home. Once you find out what the rescue group will provide, make your own list of items to purchase for your new Basenji. You can use the shopping list that

follows as a guide. You'll also find a copy of this list in Appendix C. Use the list in Appendix C to make any shopping notes you may need, and remove it from this book to take with you to the store. Remember, this list is only a suggested list. You may elect to purchase only the minimum supplies you'll need at first, and then the others as time and budget permits.

## Shopping List — Rescue Basenji

☐ Wire crate — A good wire crate size is about 30" L x 22" W x 25" H (76 cm x 56 cm x 64 cm).

☐ Travel crate *or* safety restraint harness for trips in the car — A good travel crate size is 27" L x 20" W x 19" H (69 cm x 51 cm x 48 cm); but for large Basenjis or for long trips consider the 32" L x 23" W x 23" H size (81 cm x 58 cm x 58 cm).

☐ Blankets, bed, or carpeting for crates — Ask the rescue person if the Basenji will tolerate a "doggy bed" in its crate, or if blankets or carpeting is a better idea. (Some carpeting stores will sell or give you extra carpeting samples.)

☐ Food and water dishes for inside the crate — Stainless steel is preferred.

☐ Water dish for outside the crate — Stainless steel is preferred.

☐ Collar — A good nylon or leather buckle-style collar is recommended.

☐ 6-foot (1.8 m) leash — Nylon, cotton, or leather.

☐ Retractable leash — The Flexi® 3-8, 26 foot (8 m) long, is a good one.

☐ Dog license — Remember to bring a rabies vaccination certificate and proof of spay/neuter.

☐ Identification tag — Include your name, address, city, state, phone number with area code, and the phone number to your dog's tattoo or microchip registry, and indicate that your dog is tattooed or microchipped.

☐ Plastic-coated metal wire tie out, if necessary (Something that can't easily be chewed through.)

☐ Food _____(Note brand/type that dog is currently being fed.)

☐ Vitamins _____(Note brand/type that dog is currently being given.)

☐ Treats _____(Note brand/type that dog is currently being fed. If you choose rawhide, look for rawhide made in the USA.)

☐ Chew toys, such as Nylabones , Gumabones , Kong toys, etc.

☐ "Fetch" toys, such as a rope toy or fake sheepskin toy

☐ Bitter Apple spray (If necessary to discourage chewing on houseplants and furniture.)

☐ Stain/Odor remover (Accidents do happen!)

☐ Nail clippers (If you plan to trim the dog's nails yourself.)

☐ Grooming brush, stripping comb, or hound glove

☐ Gentle pet shampoo

☐ Flea control/Heartworm preventative products — Discuss with the rescue person and your veterinarian.

☐ First aid kit for dogs

☐ Pooper scooper

☐ Magnetic latches for doggy-level cabinets

☐ Film (You'll want to take lots of pictures!)

Additional items not listed here:

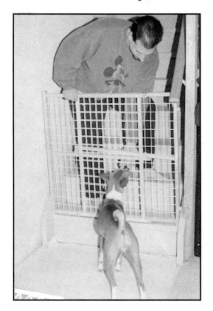

After you've done your shopping, take some time to make your home Basenji safe. Get down on your hands and knees, and try to see your home as a Basenji would see it. Are there houseplants that could be poisonous if eaten? Are there exposed electrical cords that might be good to chew on? Are there fluffy toys or pillows that would be fun to shred? Are there toilets with seats left up that would be wonderful to drink from? Are there breakable items that could fall if a table or bookcase is bumped into? If you have children, have them help by putting their toys away where Basenji teeth can't chew them.

If the rescue folks visited your home, they may have made some suggestions on how to better make your home Basenji safe. Take this well-learned advice from other Basenji owners!

Remember, it's okay to have certain rooms in your home where your new Basenji won't be allowed. Make sure that until your new Basenji is familiar with your rules and routines, the doors to these rooms are kept closed. It may also be a good idea to invest in a blanket or two to protect your furniture, since Basenjis seem to really enjoy spending time up on it, even when you don't want them to.

It's a good idea to put magnetic latches or other types of childproof latches on cabinets where household chemicals and trash containers are stored. Or, better yet, find another place to store these things. Some Basenjis will never try to get inside cabinets, but others are very adept at opening cabinets, especially if something inside smells good to them. Latches help make your cabinets harder for an inquisitive Basenji to open. Talk with your rescue person or other Basenji owners to find out what sort of latches they recommend.

You may want to consider not opening doors or windows with screens, especially if they're at or near doggy-level, or you may want to add a protective grating to low windows and to the bottom halves of doors.

Some Basenji owners have one specific place (not the crate) where they keep their Basenji's toys. This can be a basket or a box that's well within Basenji reach. If you do this, he'll soon learn where *his* toys are kept, and he'll know that anything in his box is fair game. Allowing him to have free run of his own toy box helps him learn what he's allowed to play with and chew on. If you give your Basenji his own toy box, make sure that the toy box itself is nothing your Basenji can hurt himself on if he decides to chew on it.

Plan on where you'll put your new Basenji's crate. Ideally, you'll want it to be in a location that will allow your Basenji to have quiet time. It should not be placed in direct sunlight, or in a drafty area. You may want to cover the back part of the crate with an old towel or blanket to make your dog's "den" more cozy and private. Make sure the crate is well out of reach of houseplants, curtains, and electrical cords.

Once you've done a thorough run-through of the inside of your house, it's time to take a look at the outside. If you have a fenced-in yard, you should walk the fence line and look for any openings your Basenji may be able to slip through. A good rule of thumb is that any opening larger than your fist will be a temptation for your new Basenji. You should also look for any protruding nails, sharp points of chain link, or anything else that might cause injury to your dog.

It's a good idea to look on the other side of the fence to see if there's anything that might attract your dog, such as trash or other debris that can be pulled through the fence by nimble Basenji paws. You should also inspect your yard for any poisonous plants or flowers. If you have a garden area or any other areas you don't want your Basenji to get into, be sure to fence or block them off. Basenjis love to munch on grass, so don't use fertilizers, herbicides, or insecticides in areas your Basenji will go.

Check your gate to be sure it is locked and can't be unlatched by a clever Basenji, a strong wind, or a neighborhood child. Make sure your Basenji won't have access to any outside trash containers. Garden tools, fuels, oils, and any other outdoor chemicals, such as fertilizers, should be stored out of reach.

If you don't have a fenced-in yard, be sure the area your Basenji will use outdoors is free from any poisonous plants or flowers. Again, look for anything that could cause injury to your dog. Make sure the tieout you plan on using is in good condition and is long enough to give your Basenji plenty of room to roam, but short enough that it doesn't get tangled or wrapped around any trees, lightposts, or other objects. You also want to make sure your Basenji won't have access to any outside trash containers. Again, garden tools, fuels, oils, and any other outdoor chemicals, such as fertilizers, should be stored out of reach. You may want to consider building a dog run for your pet, especially if your yard isn't, or can't be, fenced.

If you have a pool or a hot tub, you'll want to take measures to keep your new Basenji away from these doggy-dangers. You don't want your new Basenji to drink the chemically treated water from pools or hot tubs, and you don't want him falling in and drowning. Basenjis don't usually enjoy getting wet, but they are curious and could easily fall into a pool or uncovered hot tub and drown, because they either can't swim or don't know the way out.

If your Basenji will be spending time with you around a pool, hot tub, lake, or other body of water, you may be able to teach him how to swim and get to safety if he should fall in. Talk to your rescue person and other Basenji owners for more information on this.

Do your best to make your house as safe as possible for your new Basenji, so that when you bring him home he can explore without you having to worry. Don't be surprised if your new Basenji finds some things that you've missed!

## *Tailtip – Traveling Safely with Your Basenji*

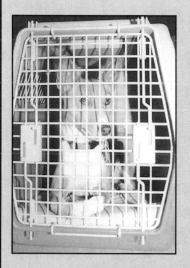

You know how important it is to wear your safety belt while riding in your vehicle. But do you realize how important it is that your dog be properly restrained while in your vehicle?

When you ride in a car, you're moving at the same speed as the car is. If the car stops suddenly, your safety belts keep you from continuing to move forward with the momentum that you had when the car was still moving. If you weren't wearing the safety belts, you'd probably end up hitting something inside the car when it stopped. The same thing is true for your dog.

Think of how many times you've seen a dog riding loose in a car or in the back of a pickup truck. Imagine what would happen if the vehicle were to stop suddenly. Just like you would hit something inside the vehicle, so would the dog. Or, even worse, the dog that was riding in the back of the pickup truck could be thrown from the truck. In either case, the message is the same — if you don't properly restrain your dog in your vehicle, he can be hurt or even killed in a sudden stop or crash. Properly restraining your dog also means that your dog can't jump out and possibly end up getting hit by another car.

Here's something else you may not have thought about. In a sudden stop or crash, an unrestrained dog could strike people who are riding in the vehicle. If this happens, the driver could lose control and people could be injured. For your dog's safety and for the safety of everyone in the vehicle, it just makes good sense to restrain your dog whenever he rides with you.

Just as there are safety devices like safety belts and air bags to protect people in vehicles today, there are things available to help protect your dog when he rides with you.

A travel crate is one way to properly restrain your dog. Travel crates come in sizes to fit every dog. If your dog travels inside a crate, he can't hit the inside of your vehicle if you stop suddenly. And, a travel crate gives your dog his own space inside your car, which is especially helpful on long trips.

Another bonus to using a travel crate is that it saves wear and tear on the inside of your car — you won't have dog hair all over the seat, and you won't have to clean the seat if your dog should get carsick. An important thing to remember with crates is that they must be secured in your vehicle so they can't move around in a crash or sudden stop.

Another good way to restrain your dog is to use a special harness that is designed to work with the safety belt system in your vehicle. Some of these harnesses have a special latch plate that fastens right into the buckle on your vehicle's safety belt, and some work by running the safety belt through the dog's harness. The harness is designed to work for your dog just like the safety belt in your vehicle works for you. It allows your dog to have some free movement, but helps keep him in place. If you use a harness, it's a good idea to put your dog in the back seat, especially if you have a vehicle that has an air bag for the right front passenger. You may also want to put a blanket or towel on the seat to protect it from dog hair and other wear and tear.

Pickup trucks present special problems for dog owners. However, there are many types of harnesses and restraint systems available today just for dogs who must ride in the beds of pickup trucks. Keep in mind that your dog can be injured by road debris while he's back in the pickup bed. The safest place for your dog may be properly restrained in the cab of the truck with you, but if you must have your dog ride in the bed of your pickup truck, make sure he's properly restrained so he can't jump out or be thrown from the vehicle in a sudden stop or crash.

If you put your dog's crate in the bed of the pickup truck, make sure it's secure so that it can't move around, and place it as far forward as you possibly can. You may also want to cover it with a blanket or tarp to keep out dust, wind, and debris.

Just as you take precautions to protect yourself when you ride in a vehicle, you should take precautions to protect your dog, too!

# Section 9. Welcome Home!

Well, the long-anticipated day has finally arrived! By adopting a rescue Basenji, you're giving a homeless dog a new chance at a wonderful life — with you! There are a few things you'll want to keep in mind as your new Basenji gets acquainted with you and your home.

Your rescue person may ask you to come and pick up your new Basenji, in which case you should be prepared with a leash, ID tags, and collar, as well as a crate or safety restraint harness for you new Basenji's ride home. Or, your rescue person may decide to bring your Basenji to your home instead. Either way, this is the time when all your paperwork should be completed, and you should be prepared to pay the adoption fee.

You may want to plan on bringing your Basenji home on a weekend — perhaps on a Friday evening or a Saturday morning. That way you and your Basenji will be able to get to know each other better without the stress of you having to get up the next morning for work. Because you have done all of your planning, preparing, and shopping in advance, you should be ready to relax and enjoy your new arrival as he investigates your home and yard.

In many ways, bringing home a rescue is a lot like bringing home a puppy. You, your family, your home, and everything about you will be all new to the rescue. Your rescue won't know the rules of your house or what to expect from you. However, what makes bringing home a rescue very different from bringing home an eight-week-old puppy is that a rescue brings with it a history and a predetermined set of expectations about people, situations and the environment based on its past experiences.

A rescued dog can be complex in many ways. For instance, your new dog may have had a lamp fall on it at one time in its life, and you might discover that it's afraid of your floor lamp. Maybe your new dog's former owner was a man who shouted a lot. That would explain why your rescue may shy away from men when they speak or make sudden moves. It may have been okay to dig at the rug and chew on furniture where your rescue came from, but you don't find that behavior acceptable. You'll need to be understanding, sympathetic; yet firm with your new dog. He'll be learning about you and your home just as you'll be learning about him, and developing the bond of trust is essential.

It's a good idea to let your new Basenji get acquainted with its new home without having a lot of company visit the first few days. As eager as you may be to have your Basenji meet your friends, allow the dog some time to settle in. Keep in mind that, just as you are getting to know your dog, your dog is getting to know you and your home.

Your Basenji may be somewhat overwhelmed by his new surroundings and new routine, and he may be a bit edgy or seem to tire easily. He may not be very hungry for a couple of days, but don't worry. Just try to maintain the diet and feeding schedule your Basenji is used to, and he'll eventually come around!

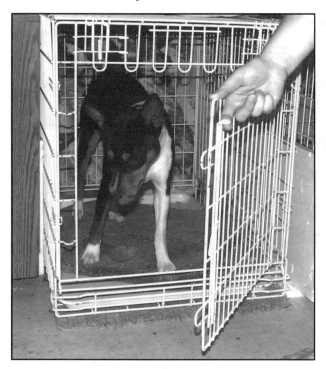

Show your new Basenji where his crate is, and leave the door open for him. Once he's had a chance to explore his surroundings and is more comfortable in your home, begin locking him in his crate for increasingly longer periods of time. You may find that your dog feels more secure in his crate — it is, after all, his "home" or "den" — and he may welcome some quiet time. Make sure he doesn't have to go potty before you put him in his crate, and give him a treat and some chew toys to keep himself occupied. If your new Basenji has been crate trained, you shouldn't have any problems. If he hasn't been crate trained, it may be challenging, but it's worth the effort.

Ignore him if he carries on while in his crate. (You don't want to reinforce that kind of behavior!) Just keep him in for a predetermined period of time, and then let him out without any fanfare.

You should also show your new Basenji the door you'll be using when he has to go outside, and take him out frequently the first few days. He may not be sure where to go when he has to go potty, and he may have a few accidents in the house. If you're lucky enough to catch him in the act, surprise him by correcting him with a loud "No!" Then calmly show him the proper place to go and reinforce the proper behavior. But the best way to teach the potty routine to your new Basenji is through repetition: Go to the door, reinforce his interest with a command like "Go potty" or "Outside," and let him out or bring him out with you. You may want to hang jingle bells on the door and ring them before the dog goes outside. Eventually, he'll learn how to let you know when he has to go!

The first several times you let your dog run loose in your fenced-in yard or tie him out, spend time with him. Keep your new Basenji company and keep him occupied so he won't be tempted to roam or get into trouble. Inside or out, a bored Basenji is a Basenji about to find trouble. The last thing you want is for your new dog to pick up some new bad habits (like fence climbing or digging) right away!

Since you've probably met your new Basenji a few times prior to bringing him home, your relationship with him should be well on its way to a good start. Change is stressful for dogs as well as humans, and after your Basenji has had some time to settle in, he'll be more confident with his surroundings and more relaxed.

## *Tailtip – Introducing Your Rescue Basenji to Other Dogs*

There are many fine books and articles on dog training and socialization, and if you're planning to add a second dog to your household, it's a good idea to read up on how to do it properly. Whether there's already a dog living with you, or whether your rescue Basenji will be the only dog in your home, it's good to know how to introduce your dog to other dogs.

Your rescue person should be an excellent source of information and should know how your rescue Basenji behaves around other dogs. While some people would argue that Basenjis aren't really good about meeting new dogs, there are others who will tell you that, even though Basenjis can put on a good show when they have a mind to, they are in general good with other dogs.

The best advice anyone can give you is that each Basenji (and each dog your Basenji will meet) is an individual, and each individual will react to a new dog in its own way. This is especially true about rescues because they have a history behind them, and no one can say for certain how your rescue will react to a new dog in *every* situation.

If you currently own a dog, make every effort to introduce your dog to the rescue Basenji you're considering before you adopt. Already having made the commitment to adopt before introducing the two dogs is a big gamble — the rescue may not get along with your dog, or your dog may not get along with the rescue. Your rescue person should be willing to take the time to allow any rescue you're thinking of adopting to meet your current dog. If they aren't willing, or seem reluctant to do so, don't be afraid to go elsewhere to adopt. The success of an adoption depends a lot on how well the rescue group is willing to work with you, and if you have another dog already, your adoption will have a better chance of succeeding if you get the cooperation you need to make it work.

Don't be afraid to change your mind about adopting any particular rescue Basenji if you discover that your dog won't tolerate the other dog in your house. Be glad you took the time up front to find out — you'll have saved yourself and the rescue dog from a lot of stress and grief. You may also discover that the rescue you want to adopt wants nothing to do with your current dog. Remember that just because those two don't seem to get along, it doesn't mean that another dog won't work out just fine.

Experts recommend that a good way to introduce two dogs to each other is on neutral territory. Neutral territory could be a park, a neighbor's backyard (get permission first!) or a parking lot. Walk the two dogs around, and give them a good chance to check each other out at a distance. Keep the dogs separated at first, but don't use the leashes to hold the dogs back — this raises their heads to a dominant, aggressive position, and it makes each dog think that the other dog is a threat.

Trade dogs with your assistant, and walk around some more. Be sure you each give both dogs plenty of love and attention. You want them to know that you accept both of them — and that you expect them to accept each other. When the dogs seem comfortable around each other at a distance, let them get closer for some sniffing and greeting. Keep the leashes loose and try not to interfere with the dogs, unless they happen to get nasty with each other. You may be pleased to discover that after a few moments of posturing, the dogs will begin to play.

Some Basenjis put on quite a show around a new dog — the hair along their backs will stand up, and they can make some terrible noises. Other Basenjis simply take a sniff or two and are ready to play.

Some dogs will get along like they've known each other their entire lives, while others will only *tolerate* having another dog around. Keep in mind that, just like with people, not every dog your dog meets wants to become friends. Sometimes two dogs just won't get along with each other no matter what you do, and they'll have to be kept separated. Just like you and me, each dog is an individual.

It's a good idea to listen to any advice your rescue person gives you about introducing a rescue to other dogs, regardless of what the books or experts say. If anyone should know the rescue, it should be the rescue person.

# Section 10. Tomorrow and Beyond

Perhaps some of the best advice you'll get from other Basenji owners is that you need to keep your sense of humor when things seem to go wrong. While it's not a good thing that your Basenji just finished shredding an entire roll of toilet paper, you can't help but laugh as he sits there amid the shredded paper with a chunk hanging from his mouth wearing an "I don't know what you're talking about — what toilet paper?" expression on his face.

The rescue group you adopted your Basenji from is an excellent source of information, and it's a good idea to contact them with any questions you may have about your new Basenji. Also, they'll probably contact you from time to time, just to make sure things are going well.

If you're interested in a monthly publication dedicated totally to Basenjis, you may want to subscribe to *The Basenji* magazine. There you'll not only find articles, stories, and pictures of Basenjis, but you'll also find advertisements for Basenji-related "stuff." Other dog-related magazines may also be of interest to you, including *Dog World* and *Dog Fancy*, and the *AKC Gazette*. See Appendix A of this handbook for a comprehensive Basenji-related bibliography.

You may want to join a Basenji club in your area. By attending club meetings and events, you'll get a chance to meet other folks who live with and love Basenjis, and you'll have plenty of opportunities to trade Basenji stories. Often listening to these stories makes you realize your Basenji isn't "bad" at all; he's just doing what Basenjis do! Another good reason for joining a local Basenji club is that you can pick up training tips and perhaps even get your Basenji involved in the many activities and fun matches that these clubs hold.

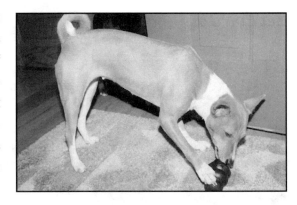

You may also want to join a national club such as the Basenji Club of America (BCOA). For information on joining the BCOA, go to the BCOA web site. See "Basenjis on the Internet" in Appendix A of this handbook for the web site address.

There are several Basenji-related electronic mailing lists on the Internet. These lists are another good place to swap Basenji stories and get answers to Basenji-related questions. You'll find the information you'll need to subscribe in the "Basenjis on the Internet" section of Appendix A.

A search for "Basenji" information on the World Wide Web will turn up many Basenji-related web sites, and you can learn a lot about the breed from those sites. The web sites listed in Appendix A are also good starting points because they have many links to other Basenji-related web sites.

If you decide to take your Basenji to obedience classes, you should do so with a good sense of humor! Basenjis are extremely intelligent and can quickly become bored with too much training all at one time. You may find that your Basenji will sit, stay, and heel beautifully in your own backyard; but get him into a class with other dogs, and he suddenly forgets everything he knows and becomes the class clown. Be firm yet fair with your Basenji, and he'll respect you for it.

One thing your Basenji is sure to enjoy is long walks — whether in a park or just around the block. There are so many interesting things to sniff and see! Just remember to be a responsible dog owner, and carry with you bags to pick up after your dog. You may find that people often stop to ask you what kind of dog you have, and you'll sometimes meet people who have owned or known a Basenji sometime in their lives. Basenjis are great conversation starters!

People often remark that their rescue Basenjis seem to truly appreciate their new homes and owners. Basenjis end up sleeping in beds, sharing tidbits from dinnertime meals, and in general become an integral part of the family. A Basenji is always a great pick-me-up after a long day at work, and he won't mind at all if you need him to dry your tears. He'll be there to lick you dry when you step out of the shower, and he may even steal your towel and enjoy a good roll in it! He'll help you find tissues that you'd forgotten between the cushions of your sofa, and he'll be glad to cuddle up with you on cold nights.

Once you've lived with and loved a Basenji, you'll find that you won't ever want to be without one. Don't be surprised if you come home from work one day and are greeted not only by a frantically wagging tail and prancing Basenji-feet, but also with a hearty "BAROOOOOOOOOOOOOOOOOOOOO!" It's just your Basenji's way of telling you that he loves you!

On the next few pages you'll find four tricks that you can teach your Basenji. These tricks are: Sit, Down, Stay, and Bang! We recommend that you teach your Basenji these tricks in the order they are listed here, because by linking the first three together, you can teach your Basenji the fourth very easily! We call these commands "tricks" because that's exactly what they are. Training your dog is really teaching him tricks!

When you're teaching your Basenji a new trick, it's a good idea to find a quiet room where there won't be any distractions. You want your Basenji to focus on you. Keep the training sessions short — no more than ten minutes at a time. If things don't seem to be going right, take a break! Training should be a fun thing that you and your Basenji do together — not a chore. Treats are used in training to help encourage your Basenji to perform the commands. When you first begin teaching your Basenji a new trick, you may find that you need to use a lot of treats in order to get him to perform.

As your Basenji learns the tricks, use treats less frequently and reward him mostly with praise. As we've mentioned several times before, you'll need a sense of humor when training your Basenji, since he may have other ideas about learning!

You'll want your Basenji to wear his collar and a six-foot leash when you're teaching him these tricks. We also recommend that the treats you use in training be something extra special, such as freeze-dried liver or some other type of doggie delight. Save these special treats only for training sessions and for when you're asking your Basenji to perform in front of your friends. You'll want to reward your Basenji with small pieces, not huge chunks. Use treats that your Basenji can easily devour in one bite. That way, he'll be listening to you and ready for the next lesson instead of being distracted by crunching down a large doggie cookie.

Once your Basenji has mastered these tricks, you can certainly continue on and teach him others. There are many fine training books that will help you teach your Basenji advanced tricks, and you may want to join a training class. Good luck!

### Teach Your Basenji "SIT"

Items required:

- Basenji

- Treats

- Leash and Collar

Time required:
Ten minutes a day until mastered

SIT is a very easy command to teach your Basenji. In fact, he may already know it. As with any training, make sure that you and your Basenji are in a location free of distractions, and keep the sessions brief. If things don't seem to be going right, take a break!

1. Hold the treat in one hand above your Basenji's nose.

2. Move your hand forward and up so that your Basenji follows it with his nose, and say the word "SIT" in a firm voice. Many Basenjis will sit at this point. If he sits, give him the treat and lots of praise.

3. If your Basenji doesn't sit, hold the treat again as in Step 1, but this time make the hand motion, say "SIT" in a firm voice, and with your other hand gently guide his rear to a sitting position. Reward him with the treat and lots of praise.

The idea here is to get your Basenji to follow your hand motion to a sitting position. As he learns the trick, keep making the hand motion further and further away from him. The hand motion will become as much of a cue as the command is.

Practice this with your Basenji until he gets the hang of it.

## *Teach Your Basenji "DOWN"*

Items required:

- Basenji

- Treats

- Leash and Collar

Time Required:
Ten minutes a day until mastered

The DOWN command is easy for your Basenji to learn, especially if he has mastered SIT. As with any training, make sure that you and your Basenji are in a location free of distractions, and keep the sessions brief. If things don't seem to be going right, take a break!

1.  Give your Basenji the SIT command and hand motion to place him in a sitting position.

2.  With the treat in your hand, make a downward motion so that your Basenji follows the hand with the treat. At the same time, say "DOWN" in a firm voice. Your Basenji may lay down at this point. If he does, give him the treat and lots of praise.

3.  If your Basenji doesn't lay down, hold the treat again in front of his nose, make the downward motion, say "DOWN" in a firm voice, and at the same time use your other hand to gently guide him into the DOWN position. Give him the treat and lots of praise.

Just like with SIT, you want your Basenji to follow your hand motion to the DOWN position. Eventually you should be able to get your Basenji to respond to the command and the downward hand motion when you're standing up straight.

Practice this with your Basenji until he gets the hang of it.

### Teach Your Basenji "STAY"

Items required:

- Basenji

- Treats

- Kitchen Chair

- Leash and Collar

Time Required:
Ten minutes a day until mastered

STAY is probably one of the most valuable things you can teach your Basenji. For example, if you want to go out to get your newspaper and you don't want your Basenji to run out the door, the STAY command not only makes it easy for you to go outside, but it can also save your Basenji from running out and possibly getting hit by a car!

As with any training, make sure that you and your Basenji are in a location free of distractions, and keep the sessions brief. If things don't seem to be going right, take a break!

1. Place a kitchen chair in the middle of a room. Put your Basenji in the DOWN position between your legs, just beneath the chair. Tell him to "STAY" in a firm voice. If he doesn't move for a few seconds, tap him gently on the top of his head and say "OK," then, give him a treat and praise.

2. If your Basenji won't STAY for even a few seconds and tries to get up, quickly place your hands on his shoulders, say "NO" in a firm voice, guide him back to the DOWN position, and say "STAY" in a firm voice.

3. Repeat Step 2 several times until your Basenji learns to STAY for a few seconds and doesn't move until you tap him on his head and say "OK." Be sure to reward him after you say "OK."

4. Increase the amount of time that you keep him in the STAY position as he learns what you want him to do. Once your Basenji has mastered STAY with you sitting over him, try it from a standing position and while you walk around him. Then you can graduate him to other situations. For example, have him STAY while people walk through the room. Or, have someone else stand over him, ready to correct him with a "NO" and a gentle push back down while you give the commands from across the room.

Practice this with your Basenji until he gets the hang of it.

### Teach Your Basenji "BANG!" ("Roll Over and Play Dead")

Items required:

- Basenji

- Treat

- Leash and Collar

Time required:
Ten minutes a day

In order to teach your Basenji this trick, he must have already mastered the SIT, DOWN, and STAY commands. This is a neat trick for your Basenji to know — he will certainly ham it up for his audience! It may take a lot of practice to get your Basenji to perform this trick correctly, but be patient. The results are well worth the work! As with any training, make sure that you and your Basenji are in a location free of distractions, and keep the sessions brief. If things don't seem to be going right, take a break!

1.  Have your Basenji SIT.

2.  With a treat in your hand, guide him to the DOWN position. With the treat still in your hand, make a motion back toward his rear so that his head follows the treat around toward his rear.

3.  When his head is turned to the side with the treat, try to get your Basenji to roll onto his other side. If he rolls, give him the STAY command, and reward him with the treat and lots of praise.

4. If your Basenji won't roll over, you may have to encourage him to do so with a gentle push using your other hand. This part may take some time, but be patient.

Once you get your Basenji to follow through to the STAY on his side, begin to use the word BANG! and the hand motion to guide him. Once he gets the hang of it, all you'll need to do is say BANG! and make a circular hand motion. Your Basenji will do the rest!

## *Tailtip – The Importance of Routines*

If you stop to think about it, a large part of your day is made up of routines. You know what time of day to have breakfast, lunch, and dinner. You know what part of your day will be spent at work and what part will be spent at home. You know when bedtime is, and you know when it's time to wake up. Just as routines are important to you as you conduct your daily business, so too are routines important to your dog.

When adopting a rescue, it's important to consider your daily routine, and how it may have to change when your new dog comes to live with you. And, you shouldn't forget that your rescue dog has been living in a home other than your own, and he'll have to learn your routine when he moves in.

We don't always like it when our routines have to change. For example, if you woke up this morning to find that your power was out, how different would things be for you? You'd most likely find some ingenious ways to adapt to being without electricity. You might light a candle so that you could see, and you'd have to do without your electric razor.

You may even go out for breakfast because your toaster wouldn't be working. At any rate, you can see how a change in routines affects your life.

Now, imagine how things would have to change when you bring your rescue Basenji home.

Taking the time to envision how you would have to alter your daily routines *before* you adopt a rescue Basenji will make the experience less stressful for you and for your new friend. If you plan ahead, the changes will be expected and will go smoothly — they won't show up later as surprises. For example, you may have to get up earlier than normal so you can let your Basenji out in the morning, and you may find that you can't just relax and sit down to watch TV in the evening because your Basenji wants to play!

We've seen how your daily routines would change, but what about your new Basenji's routines? Your rescue Basenji is probably used to getting up and going to bed at certain times, and he's probably used to being fed and played with at other times. Your dog is comfortable with his routines, just like you are with yours.

Disturbing your dog's routines can be stressful; but, as we've mentioned before, your Basenji is flexible and will adapt to life with you. Once again, planning ahead is the key to making the transition from the rescue home to your home less stressful for your dog.

Before you adopt a Basenji, discuss with your rescue person what sort of routines the dog is currently used to and how best to make the transition to your routines. Your rescue person may agree to help you out by slightly altering the dog's routines for a few days before he goes home with you, so that his routines are closer to your own. Again, you'll have to be flexible and understand that not only is this a major change for you, but it is a major change for your dog as well.

You should make arrangements with your rescue contact to meet the rescue Basenji you are considering several times. This way, you and the dog can get to know each other. Your rescue person may also allow you to take the rescue out for walks or out for an afternoon.

Spend quality time getting to know the dog you're considering so, when it comes time for him to come home with you, you'll already be off to a good start. The rescue person may want to visit your home with the rescue dog, and you should encourage at least two or three such visits so the rescue will find your home a familiar and welcoming place.

When your dog comes home, you can expect a transition period that will be somewhat stressful for him as he gets used to his new life and new routines. Don't try to make drastic changes right away with your new dog. Expect that he may not want to eat very much for the first few days, and he may even have an accident or two in the house. This is all normal, and in time the dog will adjust.

Your rescue person should be glad to help you with any questions you may have during the transition period. Rest assured that if you've planned ahead, the adjustment period will be much shorter, and the stress will be lessened for both you and your new dog.

# Section 11. Top 10 Mistakes You Don't Want to Make

**Mistake #1: Ignore the advice of your rescue person.**

You'd be amazed at how many rescue people sit up nights, pulling out their hair, just because the adoptive family won't take their advice. The advice is there for a reason — and that reason is to make your adoption experiences as smooth and trouble-free as possible. Your rescue person wants to support you and provide you with tips on how to deal with the situations and problems that may arise with your dog. He or she has a good working knowledge of the breed and knows pretty well what works and what won't. If you want to set your rescue experience up to fail, then you'll most likely want to ignore whatever your rescue person says. But, if you're dedicated to your new dog and really want the adoption to work out, heed the advice you're given. You and your new dog will be much happier, and your adoption will have a greater chance of being successful!

## Mistake #2: Keep thinking that you know it all.

Being a know-it-all can be a dangerous occupation, and it goes hand in hand with Mistake #1. There's no better way for an adoption to fail than to believe that you've seen it all and know how to handle every situation that may arise. Even people who have bred and owned dogs for years still find there's always something they didn't know, and they make it a point to keep on learning. After all, there's no such thing as a stupid question. If you don't know or don't understand something, go right ahead and ask! It's better to ask questions and learn the answers than to spend time wondering and making mistakes that could easily be avoided.

## Mistake #3. Think of your newly adopted dog as a "second class" or "throwaway" dog.

Believe it or not, people can and do think this way about dogs that others have given up. It's a sad fact, but just simply being a "secondhand" or "rescue" dog changes people's perception of what the dog is worth. It's a mindset that many people inadvertently go into an adoption with, thinking in the back of their minds that because someone else didn't want the dog, there must be something wrong with it. While in commercial monetary terms your rescue dog may not be championship material, realize that the love and respect you share with him is priceless. This may sound a little preachy, but if you stop to think about it, you'll realize it's true — each and every rescue dog, regardless of its past, is worthy of all the love, support, and caring you can possibly give it. After all, your rescue dog looks to you for these things, and he's eager to give you lots of love in return.

## Mistake #4. Don't ever crate your dog.

There are circumstances when you wouldn't want to crate your dog, and situations in which you may not feel you need to crate it. But leaving your rescue home alone uncrated is trouble waiting to happen. If your new dog comes to you already crate-trained and you don't keep at it, you could be undoing all the hard work that someone did. It sometimes takes a great deal of time and effort to crate train. By not crating your dog (especially if he's already used to it), you're doing him a disservice, too. Imagine how much trouble an unsupervised dog can get into — and imagine what a bored or restless dog will do to your furniture, floors, or other prize possessions if he's left

uncrated. It's a general rule of thumb that your dog will be safer and happier if you crate him. Rescue dogs have been returned to rescue because their adoptive families didn't bother to keep them crated when no one was home, and the families actually blamed the dog when it got into the garbage, hopped up on a table or countertop, or "ate" a sofa cushion. Do your dog a favor — remove the temptation by keeping him in his crate when he can't be supervised! For more information on crates and crate training, see the Tailtip on crate training after Section 6 in this handbook.

## Mistake #5.  Let your dog get away with "it."

"It" can be anything — from begging at the table to getting into the trash to not wanting to move when he's sleeping in your favorite chair. Remember, dogs are pack animals and they naturally will look to you for leadership. If no leadership is forthcoming, they'll assume that they must be the leader, and that's where the trouble starts. Before you even bring your new dog home, sit down with the people you live with and make a list of what the dog will and won't be allowed to do. Be realistic, and include on your list such things as which rooms or furniture the dog will have access to, and whether or not you'll need to keep your trash bin tucked away or your bathroom doors closed. This way, you establish the rules ahead of time and everyone knows what the rules are, so there are no mixed signals being given to your new dog. And, once you've made the rules, be sure to be fair and enforce them. Dogs aren't dummies — from time to time they will test the waters and challenge your authority. If you are fair, firm and consistent, you and your new dog will be much happier.

## Mistake #6.  Believe in the "My Dog is Perfect and Doesn't Need Any Training" Syndrome.

This is one disease you won't want to catch. Dogs are like us in so many ways — we have a need to keep on learning and expanding our knowledge, and so do they. Sharing your life with a dog means sharing experiences and teaching your dog new things. Training doesn't have to be anything on a grand scale — take the time to teach your dog to "shake hands," roll over, fetch — whatever you want. A large part of a successful human-dog relationship lies in the amount of time you spend together. Take the time and teach your dog a trick or two — you'll both benefit!

**Mistake #7. Don't establish and stick to a schedule.**

Remember the Tailtip on the importance of routines after Section 10 in this handbook? If you don't, you might want to take a quick peek at it. Think of how inconvenient things can be if *your* routine is disturbed. Now, think of it from your dog's perspective. He lives for routine — he knows what time you get up in the morning, he knows when it's time to eat, and he expects these events to take place day after day, unfailingly. While it's not realistic to expect that your routine will never vary, it's a good idea to get your dog into a fairly well established routine and stick with it as best you can. By doing so, you can help eliminate a lot of anxiety and frustration your dog may experience if he's not on any sort of schedule at all.

**Mistake #8. Expect life with your new dog to be perfect — always.**

Looking at an adoption through rose-colored glasses is an easy trap to fall into. After all, you're giving a homeless dog a wonderful chance at a new life — with you! The pre-adoption expectations of many people are often rosy, and it can come as an unpleasant surprise when their dog doesn't fit their expectations right away. Remember, while dogs are flexible, change can be as difficult for them as it can be for you. Don't be discouraged if your dog has accidents in the house the first week or so, or if things don't go smoothly right away. With any adoption or change there's an adjustment period, and you need to be aware of it and be ready to deal with whatever problems may arise. Having realistic expectations can help make your adoption experience much, much smoother.

## Mistake #9.  If it doesn't work out, I can simply exchange the dog I've adopted for another.

If you ask a rescue group to do this, don't be surprised if "No!" is their response. If you've deceived the rescue group, or if you've gone into an adoption with the expectation that if things don't work out you'll simply be given dog after dog until you are happy, you may find you're sorely mistaken! Granted, sometimes people/dog matches don't work out, and in those cases where an honest effort has been put forth, exchanges can be considered and made. But if you're not willing to give it your all, don't adopt. Adoption is making a lifelong commitment to your new dog — make sure you're committed to doing your part to make the adoption work.

## Mistake #10.  Be afraid to admit you've made a mistake.

Hey, everyone makes mistakes — everyone. If you adopt and your situation changes, or if you discover that things just aren't working out and you've given it a fair chance, don't be afraid to admit it. It's the rescue person's job when placing a dog to learn as much about you as possible, and to make sure that the placement and adoption is in both yours and the dog's best interest. If you've given it an honest effort, don't feel bad about having to return a dog. Be truthful with the rescue group, and let them know what's going on. It's a risk of doing rescue work that some dogs will be returned — in fact, it's inevitable. Not every match is "made in Heaven," but for both the sake of the dog and you, if things aren't working out, make your rescue person aware of the situation. They'll do whatever they can to help you out.

# Tailtip – Canine Courtesy

It's a warm spring day and you and your Basenji are out for a walk in the park. To your left, children are playing on swings, and some are tumbling and rolling on the ground.

Your Basenji is suddenly on the alert — a large black dog has just run through the crowd of children and is heading right toward you. No matter that the dog stops just short of your dog and play bows, tail wagging in a friendly manner.

As its breathless owner apologizes for the fact that his dog has just frightened you, you turn to leave and discover that you just stepped in a pile of doggy-doo that some other careless dog owner didn't bother to pick up when his dog left it behind. Your wonderful afternoon at the park suddenly has become a bad memory. Seem far fetched? Maybe, but the truth of the matter is, stories like this one, true or not, are giving dogs a bad rap.

Cities across the country are passing very strict ordinances regarding dogs in city parks. These cities feel strict ordinances are necessary because too many people ignore the signs requiring them to keep their dogs on leashes and clean up after their dogs. All too often, the irresponsible dog owners ruin it for the responsible owners. In fact in one city, if you want to walk your dog in any city park, you must apply for a permit which costs $40.00 a year (for up to two dogs). You must renew this permit every year, and you must carry it with you while you're in the park. Your dog must be on a leash, and the leash cannot be longer than six feet. You must also carry bags for picking up after your dog. If you're stopped and asked, you must produce not only your permit but the bags as well. If you violate any of the rules, you can be fined.

The moral of the story:

## *Be courteous, follow the rules, and clean up after your dog!*

Murphy's law is that your dog will do its business while you are out on a walk or at some other inappropriate time. However, you can't always get your dog to "go potty" before you leave home, and you can't always control where your dog will want to do its business. I've had one of my dogs do its business on the sidewalk on a busy corner — right in front of a police car that was stopped for the traffic light! As long as you clean up after your dog, no one will say a word — you are being responsible! I often tell people not to worry if their dog goes on the neighbor's lawn while they're out on a walk — just so long as you pick it up!

Keeping your dog on a leash is also very important. For one thing, most cities have leash laws. These laws are designed not only to protect the public from loose dogs, but they are also intended to protect your dog! If you've ever been out walking your dog (on a leash) when an unleashed dog approached, you know what I mean. And, imagine what could happen if your unleashed dog decides to run off into the street and how terrible you'd feel if he got hit by a car! The moral of this story:

### *Keep your dog on a leash!*

Responsible dog owners are courteous dog owners. It doesn't take much to be courteous, and it really pays off!

# Section 12. When Things Don't Go Smoothly: Dealing with Some Common Problems

Nowhere is it written that life is supposed to be fair or simple. This certainly goes for life with a Basenji — or, for that matter, any breed of dog or type of pet. Taking on the responsibility of a pet is a commitment you make to the pet for its lifetime. That can be a long time, and it's inevitable that somewhere along the way a problem or two may surface. We've gathered the following questions from folks who have encountered some common dog-related problems, and we've compiled some general advice on dealing with those problems.

In any circumstance where you feel you're unable to deal with a problem relating to your dog, consult a professional dog trainer, animal behaviorist, or veterinarian. These professionals are best suited to helping you work through dog-related problems.

**Q: My dog is very possessive of his toy/rawhide/crate/food/etc. He growls at anyone who comes near. What can we do about this?**

**A**: This type of protectiveness is a common problem many dog owners face. By growling, your dog is telling you he thinks he's the boss, and he thinks you should let him have his way. One thing you should never do is to push the dog in this situation — you could end up being bitten. It's a better idea to try to figure out what types of things your dog is possessive with, and then work on correcting the problem. Especially for first-time dog owners, situations like this can be frightening and stressful for the whole family. You'll want to consult a professional dog trainer or animal behaviorist to help you work this problem through. In the meantime, you and others in your household should avoid situations that are known to set the dog off. If possible, avoid giving your dog the things he tends to be possessive of, especially items such as rawhide bones. Or, give him those things only when he's in his crate. If your dog growls when he's up on your bed, don't let him up there anymore. Another tactic is to work around the situation by asserting your dominance without having a full-blown confrontation. For example, if he growls at you when you try to take food away, distract him from the food with a toy, then remove the food.

**Q: My dog is always getting into the trash! Just last week he got sick from eating something he found in there. What can I do to keep him from raiding the garbage?**

**A:** Some dogs never touch the trash, while others think it's their own personal feast. In any case, there can be tempting and sometimes dangerous things lurking in the garbage. Your best bet is to make it impossible for your dog to access the trash. Put your waste can behind a cabinet door and install a childproof lock on that door. Or, if this isn't practical, purchase a trash bin with a secure lid, or place your trash bin up on a countertop, out of the dog's reach. Don't just make it difficult for your dog to get into the trash because he may just rise to the challenge, and you'll be back to square one again before you know it!

**Q: This is the third pair of socks/underwear/etc. the dog has chewed holes in! What can I do to keep this from happening again?**

**A:** The answer here is quite simple — make it impossible for your dog to get hold of these objects! Get in the habit of putting clothing away out of your dog's reach. Consider investing in a laundry hamper or basket, and make sure your dog can't get to it.

**Q: I'm running out of tissues and/or toilet paper! Every time I turn my back, my dog is shredding or unraveling the stuff!**

A: Like in the two previous questions, the secret to success is making it impossible for your dog to get into trouble in the first place. Place tissue boxes up out of reach, or hide them inside cabinets. If your Basenji figures this out, install a childproof lock on the cabinet door. Hang toilet paper rolls so they unroll towards the wall — this makes it more difficult for your dog to unravel it — and try to keep the bathroom doors closed.

**Q: Things were going so well for us until I started letting my dog sleep on the bed! Now he thinks he can go up there anytime he wants, and he growls at us when we try to make him leave.**

A: The pack mentality strikes again! Dogs look for a leader — and the leader gets privileges (such as sleeping up on the bed). If your dog doesn't see you as the leader, he will tend to assume that it's *his* job, and that's when problems start. Nip this problem in the bud by not allowing your dog to sleep with you (he has his own crate anyway, right?). If you must have him up on the bed, do so with the mutual understanding that he has to leave whenever you tell him to — and leave willingly, without complaints. Basic obedience training is an excellent way to instill yourself as the leader in your dog's eyes, and if you are fair and consistent with your commands and expectations, your dog will understand what's expected of him and comply when you ask.

**Q: I can't seem to keep my dog in the yard! He keeps climbing the fence/going under the fence and I'm afraid he'll get lost or hit by a car!**

**A:** Often, these "escape artists" are a difficult lot to live with. For whatever reason, they aren't content in their own yards and think life outside the boundaries is much more exciting. In dealing with an escape artist, you'll first want to try to figure out why he's trying to leave. Is he bored from being left alone in the yard for long periods of time? Are there other dogs or people outside of your yard he's trying to play with? If your dog goes under fences, you'll want to invest some time and effort into making it difficult for him to do so. You can bury chicken wire 6 inches (15 cm) or so under the soil to help deter his digging. Block off any holes that he's been sticking his head through. Many folks will tell you that if a dog can't see what's on the other side of the fence, he'll be less likely to want to go over and investigate. You can try blocking your dog's view of the other side with shrubbery, a wooden fence, or some other visual barrier. If you have a chain link fence and a dog that likes to climb it, you may need to install a taller solid fence. Or, you may want to try installing a radio fence a foot (30 cm) or so around the inside perimeter, thereby deterring the dog from even getting close to the fence. *Whatever you do, if you have a dog that likes to escape, don't ever leave him alone in the yard unsupervised, even if he's on a tieout! A dog on a tieout can be seriously injured or even killed if he gets hung up on something or stuck!*

**Q: I left my dog out while I went away to work and he's gone and chewed things up! Now I have to buy a new sofa/chair/blanket/etc. Can I make him stop doing this?**

**A:** If your dog can't be trusted loose and alone in the house, then by all means, don't leave him loose! The crate is safest place for your dog when you aren't home or if you're busy and can't keep an eye on him. Check out the Tailtip on crating your dog (after Section 6 in this handbook) for some more information.

**Q: I've got a new boyfriend/girlfriend and my dog doesn't seem to like him/her at all. What can I do about this?**

**A:** Sometimes change is difficult for dogs to accept. If you've been his number one and suddenly someone else appears in the picture, your dog may not be getting the same amount of attention he's used to. Try getting everyone together for a fun day at the park, regular walks, and playtime activities. If your dog has had some basic obedience training, have your new partner work with your dog to help establish his "pack rank." Have your partner feed the dog, give the dog plenty of praise and treats, and in general share in the care of your pet. If, after all this, your pet still won't accept your new partner, you may need to seek professional help, or consequently end up choosing between the two.

**Q: I just caught the kids next door teasing my dog. I guess that explains why he growls when children come around. What can I do about this?**

**A:** If they've been teasing your dog for any length of time, it's no wonder he's not happy when the little ones arrive! Often, dogs who bite kids aren't bad dogs at all — they're just dogs who have been teased or hurt one too many times by kids. Bad experiences are easily remembered, and it's up to you to make sure your dog doesn't have unsupervised contact with children until you get some professional help in dealing with the problem. You don't want to risk a lawsuit if your dog should go beyond growling and nip or bite at a child. If you have children who frequently bring their friends home, enforce strict house rules about what can and cannot be done with the family dog, and make sure your dog has a "safe haven" where he can go to avoid these little visitors. See Section 7, "Children and Dogs: Knowing the Rules," for more on this. Also, you'll want to talk to your neighbors about their children's behavior. This can go a long way toward preventing even more problems down the road.

**Q: My dog just doesn't seem to be himself lately. He's hungry all the time, but he's acting lethargic. What could be wrong?**

**A:** If you notice changes in your dog's eating habits, behavior, or activity level, by all means get him into the veterinarian for an exam. Just like you and me, dogs do get sick occasionally. It's better to know what's going on with your pet and help him get back on a healthy track than to discover that you've let a health problem go for too long.

**Q: My dog really experiences separation anxiety. Whenever we leave, he screams and thrashes around in his crate, and sometimes he destroys things when we're gone. How can I make our absences less traumatic for him?**

**A:** With rescues — or for that matter, with just about any dog — separation anxiety can be present to varying degrees. Working separation anxiety out of a dog takes a lot of effort and dedication, but the results are well worth the work! For starters, you should use a sturdy, safe crate with a door that latches securely, and you should get into the habit of crating your dog every time you leave. Getting him into a routine will help him deal with some of his anxiety — doing the same thing over and over will help him understand that you aren't leaving forever. A large part of working with separation anxiety typically starts with getting the dog used to you leaving him alone in one room for a short period of time, and then gradually working up to leaving him alone in the house (crated, of course).

Some people will leave a radio or television on for the dog when they leave, just so there's some background noise in the house. You may also want to consider using "doggy day care" a few days a week to see how the dog does when left with other people and dogs.

If your dog seems to be experiencing separation anxiety, you can also ask your rescue person for some tips or recommendations that he or she may have had success in using. For severe cases of separation anxiety, your best bet may be to get with a trainer or animal behaviorist to help work with your dog and you.

**Q: My dog seems to have two speeds — sleep and full steam ahead. He's driving me crazy, always wanting attention! What can I do?**

A: Basenjis are, by nature, very high-energy dogs. They play hard, and sleep when they're tired of playing. If your Basenji seems to want a lot of attention, you may need to stop and take an inventory of how much time you're actually spending with him. It's understandable that if you've worked all day, you'll be inclined to rest all evening — but from your dog's point of view, he's been waiting patiently all day for you, and he's ready to play! Try taking him on a nightly walk, or

engaging him in some active play or training. You may even want to consider enrolling in an obedience, flyball, or agility class just for fun. The exercise will benefit you both, and spending quality time together will help tighten the relationship between you and your Basenji.

**Q: My Basenji is an only dog. Do you think he's lonely?**

**A:** Not necessarily! Dogs are pack animals, and they easily adapt to the human family structure. If your dog seems healthy and content, and if you're giving him plenty of exercise and attention, then he may very well be happy with things they way they are. If your dog came from a place where there were other dogs around to play with, it's possible that he may be missing his canine companions. Why not take him back for a visit and some fun play? Also, enrolling him in "doggy day care" a few days a week can help fulfill his need to socialize with other canines! If you think your dog would enjoy a playmate, consider yourself first. Become more active with your pet by attending obedience, flyball, or agility classes with him. Certainly, if you're able to add a second dog to your life, consider doing so. Just don't expect your dog's new friend to satisfy his need for *your* attention.

## *Tailtip – SKUNKED! Making the Best of a Smelly Situation*

Ugh! Your Basenji is rubbing his muzzle on the ground, pawing at his face, drooling, and there's a foul odor in the air that could only be caused by one thing — a skunk! Meeting a skunk is never a pleasant experience for your pet. Whether you live out in the country or in a city suburb, chances are that sometime in your pet's life he'll encounter one of those smelly creatures. If you're lucky, getting skunked may never happen to your pet, but if it does, you'll want to act quickly to minimize the discomfort your dog will be experiencing, and, of course, the odor!

It's possible for your dog to have an adverse allergic reaction to the skunk spray, so watch for the symptoms (swelling, difficulty breathing, etc.) and contact your veterinarian immediately if they occur. You'll also want to contact your veterinarian quickly if your pet has been bitten, or you suspect your pet has been bitten, by a skunk.

When dealing with a skunk-sprayed dog, remember that whatever he touches will end up smelling skunky too (and, consequently, will require deodorizing). This means that, if at all possible, you'll want to keep your dog outdoors until after you've treated him for the skunk spray. Realize that your dog will most likely be extremely distressed by the incident, especially if he's gotten sprayed directly in his face. He'll want to rub his head and body on anything and everything (including you!) to try and get the odor off, and the last thing you want is to have him rubbing all over your carpeting or furniture.

If the dog does rub on your furniture or carpeting, there are many products on the market that can be used to safely deodorize them. Be sure to follow the instructions on the package, and be absolutely certain the product you're using is safe for the fabrics or materials you plan to use it on. Your best bet may be to contact a professional cleaning company for their advice and help.

To help deodorize your pet, the following is a list of skunk-odor treatments. Washing your dog with plain water or shampoo before using one of these treatments may "set" the odor on your dog, so you're usually best off trying one of these treatments first. With any of these treatments, several applications may be necessary to get the odor out, and you may never be able to eliminate all of the odor.

*IMPORTANT NOTE: If your pet has sensitive skin, a wound, or a rash of any type, please be sure to contact your veterinarian before attempting to use any of these treatments.*

**Tomato juice** — This traditional standby is perhaps the best known skunk-odor neutralizer. In order for tomato juice to do its job properly, you'll need to saturate your pet's skin and coat with the juice — and lots of it. Make sure you work the juice into the coat right down to the skin, paying close attention to the areas where your dog received the direct hit. These are usually the dog's face and chest (but, be sure you don't get any in his ears, eyes or nose!). Also pay close attention to the "hidden" areas, such as between your dog's toes and on his underbelly. After you've applied the juice, you'll need to wait for it to dry. Once the juice has dried, shampoo it out.

**Over-the-counter odor control products** — There are many products on the market today designed to help minimize and eliminate skunk spray odor from pets. You'll find products such as Skunk Off$^{TM}$ and Nature's Miracle$^{TM}$ at your local pet store, in dog supply catalogs, and at your veterinarian's office. If you live in an area where skunks are plentiful, you'll want to stock up on one or more of these products. Be sure to follow the instructions on the package, and be careful when using them around your dog's ears, eyes and nose.

**Homemade skunk odor control mixtures** — If you're stuck without tomato juice or an over-the-counter product, you can mix your own batch of odor control solution. Just mix together 1 quart (1 L) of 3% hydrogen peroxide, ¼ cup (60 ml) of baking soda, and 1 teaspoon (5 ml) of a mild liquid soap. Apply this to your pet, wait a few minutes, then rinse thoroughly. Again, you'll want to be careful not to get this mixture into your dog's ears, eyes or nose.

**Professional cleaning** — Many grooming shops offer de-skunking services. If you simply can't deal with deodorizing your pet yourself, you may want to look in your phone book for a groomer who advertises this service. One drawback to going this route is that the groomer may not be available when you need the service — such as late at night or early in the morning, when skunks are most active.

**Time and patience** — As wonderful as odor control products may claim to be, the best remedy of all is time and patience. No matter how diligent you are, some skunky odor can remain with your pet, but rest assured, it will fade with time!

# Section 13. Keeping Your Basenji Running Right: Maintenance Checks and Services for a Healthy Pet

A healthy Basenji is a happy Basenji! Here you'll find information and tips on how you can keep your yodeler in tip-top condition. Maintenance is all about proper care and doing your best to prevent problems before they start. If you ever have any questions about the health of your dog, remember that your veterinarian is an excellent resource! You may also find it helpful to invest in an easy-to-read, up-to-date pet medical book to help you identify and deal with some of the more common types of doggy problems.

The following covers some of the most common Basenji maintenance items you can do yourself.

# Weight

Has your Basenji been munching down too many goodies lately? Keeping your dog's weight at its proper level is one of the most important things you can do to help him maintain his health.

Female Basenjis typically weigh about 22 pounds (10 kg), while males are usually around 24 pounds (11 kg).

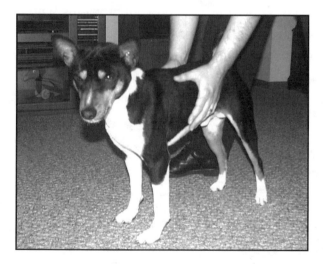

Of course, the proper weight for your dog will also be dependent upon his body structure and height. Small-boned or short dogs can weigh a bit less, large-boned or tall dogs can weigh a bit more, and well-muscled dogs can weigh more regardless of their height.

Here's a quick test you can do to see if your dog is at his proper weight:

With your Basenji standing in front of you, run your hands gently down his sides. Can you just feel his ribs?

If you can, he's most likely at his proper weight.

If you can't feel his ribs, he could probably stand to lose a bit of weight. If your dog is otherwise healthy, try cutting back on snacks and treats, and consider cutting back on his food portions, just a bit. Also, you'll want to increase his level of activity (but remember, don't over do it, especially if he's a couch potato!). Try taking longer or more frequent walks, and spend some time on activities that will keep him moving, such as chasing a ball or flying disc. You may also want to find other dog owners who are looking for playmates for their own dogs.

If you have an older dog, a dog with chronic health problems, or if your Basenji is clearly overweight, consult your veterinarian for assistance in helping your dog achieve his proper weight.

## Toenails

Many of us cringe at the thought of clipping a dog's toenails. If you'd rather not tackle this task on your own, you can have a friend, veterinarian, or local dog groomer to do it for you. But if you'd like to give toenail maintenance a try, here are some things you need to know:

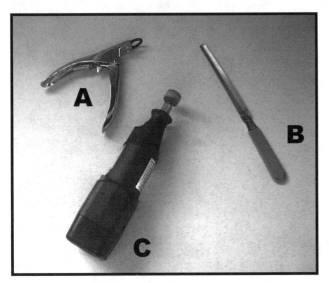

Proper equipment is essential to trimming toenails correctly. You'll want to invest in a set of nail clippers especially made for clipping dog toenails (A), and you'll need to be sure that the clipper blade is sharp. A dull blade can make toenail clipping uncomfortable for your pet. If you'd rather not use clippers, or if you'd like to round off the trimmed edges, you may want to purchase a nail file (B) or, better yet, a power toenail grinder (C).

If he isn't already used to having people touch his feet, get your dog used to having his feet handled. If your dog is touchy about his tootsies, you'll want to slowly get him used to the feel of your hands on his feet. This may take some time, so be patient and don't get discouraged.

You'll want to be able to hold his paw comfortably in your hand, and press gently but firmly on each of his toepads. Remember to praise your dog each time he allows you to do this! If your dog simply won't accept your handling of his feet, it's probably better to have a professional groomer or veterinarian do the work.

Learn the mechanics of the dog toenail. Your dog may have any combination of white, clear, and dark toenails, but they're all structured in the same way. There are two parts to the toenail: the outer, hard part which is made of dead cells and has no nerve endings; and the pink inner part which has blood vessels and nerve endings, called the "quick." When you trim a toenail, you only want to cut the tip, to just before where the quick is located. If you cut into the quick, it will bleed and your dog will feel pain. In bright light, it's easy to see where the quick is located if your dog has white or clear toenails.

If your dog has dark or black toenails, it's a lot harder (if not impossible) to see where the quick is. In that case, you'll want to be conservative and only trim a little bit off the tip, and perhaps file off the rest. Before you do any toenail trimming it's a good idea to study your dog's toenails and see where the quick is located in each one. Familiarize yourself with the way his nails look — you'll be able to easily spot any unusual changes or problems later on.

Take your time trimming the toenails, and praise your dog often. Once you've obtained the proper equipment and your dog is comfortable having his feet handled, choose a foot (one of the front feet is a good place to start). Grasp one of the toes in your hand, gently but firmly. Take your clipper and place it over the tip of the nail as shown, making sure that it's not too close to the quick. Snip off the tip of the nail. Continue on to the next nail until all are trimmed, praising your dog often. If your dog struggles, take a short break to settle him down, then continue. It may take several sessions before you've cut all the nails.

Realize that somewhere, sometime, you might slip and cut into the quick. It can and does occasionally happen. When you cut into the quick, your dog may yelp, and the nail will most likely bleed. Calm your dog and do what you can to stop the bleeding. If you have a styptic pencil or powder, you can apply it to the bleeding nail to stop the flow. If you don't have these items, you can also use cornstarch to stop the bleeding. If you've cut really deep into the quick, or if the bleeding just won't stop, contact your veterinarian immediately.

Don't worry if you are only able to do one foot, or even one toenail on your first try. Eventually, with patience and practice, both you and your dog will gain confidence and you'll get the hang of trimming toenails. If your dog seems overly upset with having his nails trimmed, you may want to have your veterinarian or professional groomer do the job.

Don't like the clippers? Try a toenail grinder! These nifty little units come in either electric or battery powered versions. You can use the grinder to round off any sharp edges on your dog's nails, or, if the nails aren't too overgrown, you can use the grinder to gently grind away at the excess toenail.

Realize that it may take your dog a while to become comfortable with the sound and feel of the grinder. Be sure to follow the instructions that came with the grinder, and be careful not to hold the grinding surface too long on your dog's nail (the grinding surface and the toenail can get too hot!). Also, it's a good idea to let the grinding surface cool off between nails.

Last, but not least, don't forget the dewclaws! Those cute little "thumbs" that some Basenjis have can quickly overgrow if not trimmed often. Trim them the same way as you would the other toenails.

# Bathing

Does the sound of running water in the tub send your Basenji into hiding? Rest assured — you're not alone! Basenjis are notorious for not liking the water, and baths certainly fall into that category.

Unless your Basenji spends a lot of time in dusty or muddy areas, you probably won't need to bathe him more than once or twice during the winter months, or once every other month during the summer. If you are allergic to pet dander, or if your Basenji has skin or coat problems, you may want to ask your veterinarian about special shampoos for these situations, and also about the frequency of bathing your dog should receive.

There's no magic trick to getting your Basenji to enjoy his baths, but there are a few things you can do to make the experience easier on yourself and on your pet.

- Before his bath, go over your pet gently with a soft brush to loosen any dirt from his coat.

- Get the bathwater running, and make sure it's warm, but not overly so. Unless there's no other way, avoid using the outside hose to bathe your Basenji — cold water doesn't feel good! You'll want to make sure the water you're using isn't too hot, either. It should be just warm to the touch. In fact, you can test the water by running it over your wrist, as you would check the temperature of a baby's bath.

- Invest in some basic items — a non-slip tub mat (to help prevent your Basenji from slipping in the tub and hurting himself), and a spray nozzle (to help rinse off the suds and direct water where you want it to go).

- Use a good quality, mild pet shampoo.

- Rinse, rinse, and rinse! Shampoo residue can irritate some dogs, so you'll want to rinse your dog thoroughly to be sure all the soap is gone from his skin and coat. A good rule of thumb is that if you think you've got it all rinsed out, rinse just one more time to be sure.

- Dry, dry, dry! Be forewarned — many Basenjis will head for the nearest piece of furniture for a good roll once they're out of the bath! Before you let your Basenji escape from the tub, dry him off as best you can with a soft towel. Don't use a blow dryer or heat lamp to dry your dog — both can cause skin irritations and burns!

- Stay away from the chills. If it's nice and warm outside, you can let your dog out into the sun to help dry off. But, be aware that even though the breeze may feel warm to you, it can be chilling to a wet dog. In many cases, it may be best to keep your dog inside and reasonably warm until he dries off completely.

# What is that sticky stuff?

It could be pine pitch, bubble gum, who knows? All you know is it's on your dog, and nothing seems to get it out! *Don't use any harsh chemicals on your pet — they can irritate his skin and cause burns!* Instead, try smearing a glob of peanut butter on the offending spot, let it sit for a few minutes, then wipe or brush off. You may have to apply the peanut butter several times to get everything out. (Slip a little dollop to your pet as a treat, if you want!) If the peanut butter doesn't seem to work, then it's time to consult your veterinarian or professional groomer for help.

# Fleas and other pests that bug us

In some areas, fleas, ticks, biting flies, and mosquitoes can be a real nuisance to you and your pet. This is one case where an ounce of prevention is truly worth a pound of cure! There are many fine products on the market designed specifically to combat these annoying critters. Your veterinarian can recommend the right product for your Basenji. There are also holistic and "natural" remedies available — check with your vet as well as other dog folks you may know before using any of these treatments on your pet.

## Brushing away dust and stress

Giving your dog a gentle going over with a soft brush or hound glove every other day will help keep him looking good, and can help your dog relax, too! This grooming time is also a fantastic opportunity to bond with your Basenji. Go ahead — have a conversation!

## And you thought they didn't shed!

Like any other creature with a furry coat, Basenjis do shed. Being blessed with a short coat, however, means that you most likely won't notice as much doggy hair around as you might with a longer coated breed. Once or twice a year, your Basenji may go through a heavy shedding cycle, commonly referred to as "blowing coat." During this time, you'll notice that there's a lot more hair coming out — you may be able to actually "pluck" hairs out. It's a good idea to invest in a good, gentle brush (not a wire one!) or a stripping knife to help remove the dead coat during this period. Whatever you use, always brush in the direction of the hair growth, never against it. The time your Basenji takes to blow his coat depends on the length of his hair, and whether or not he's grown a thick undercoat.

## Trimming the rough edges

Some Basenjis can go their entire lives without needing a trim, and others need a little touching up every now and then. If you wish, you can neaten the appearance of your Basenji's tail and trim stray hairs from underneath with a pair of scissors or clippers. Be careful not to accidentally slip and nip your pet! Also, a pair of small, blunt-nosed scissors works great for trimming whiskers.

## The ears have it

You can clean away dirt from your Basenji's ears by applying a small dab of mineral or baby oil to a cotton ball or pad, and gently swabbing the top inside part of the ears. If your Basenji needs a deeper ear cleaning, you can find many products on the market that will safely do the job. (Be sure to follow the directions on the package of any product you purchase.) Of course, you can also ask your veterinarian or professional groomer to clean your dog's ears for you.

## A million-dollar smile

Just like you, your Basenji's teeth need brushing and a good cleaning every now and then. Once again, there are many products available for cleaning dog teeth — you're sure to find something that works well for your pet. Be sure to follow the directions on the package of any product you purchase. And don't use people toothpaste — it foams too much and can make your pet ill if he should swallow it! It may take a while for your pet to get used to having his teeth brushed — be patient, gentle, and praise him often! Your veterinarian can show you how to scale minor tartar buildups from your dog's teeth, and he can professionally clean them, if necessary.

## Stop the scooting!

If your Basenji is scooting his rear end on the floor, he may have a problem with his anal glands. Your veterinarian can show you how to empty and care for these glands and, if necessary, treat any related problem.

# Routine Veterinarian Visits

Annual, semi-annual, and as-needed trips to see your veterinarian are essential to helping assure your pet is healthy. At the very least, your pet may have to see the vet once a year for his vaccinations. And, remember that your vet is your best friend whenever things aren't going well health-wise with your pet!

## Vaccinations

Your Basenji requires vaccinations at yearly intervals. These needle-pokes are essential to the health and well being of your pet, since many devastating illnesses can be prevented with them. Also, vaccinations for diseases such as rabies may be a requirement where you live, and you'll need to provide proof of vaccination before you can get a license for your pet.

## Preventing Heartworm and Other Internal Parasites

Talk with your veterinarian about the types of prevention available, and which would be most suited to your pet. Also, keep in mind that if your pet gains or loses weight that dosages may have to be adjusted — and your vet is the person who can advise you.

# Health Tests for Your Basenji

There are some breed-specific diseases that affect Basenjis, and you can perform some simple checks that can help identify if a problem may be present.

**Strip test for Fanconi Syndrome.** Purchase some glucose strips (available at your local pharmacy) for checking for glucose in the urine. Once a month, follow the directions on the package and test your pet's urine for the presence of glucose. If your dog seems to be spilling some sugar in his urine, contact your veterinarian for further evaluation of his condition. While spilling sugar isn't a sure-fire guarantee that your pet has developed Fanconi Syndrome, it's a good checkpoint and your vet will want to help you monitor your dog's health more closely if sugar is present.

**Yearly eye exam.** Certain eye diseases, such as Progressive Retinal Atrophy (PRA) and cataracts can be detected by a yearly eye exam performed by a certified canine ophthalmologist. Contact your veterinarian for the names and numbers of these doggy eye doctors in your area. Often, breed clubs will sponsor eye clinics where you can get your dog's peepers checked for a reduced fee.

**X-ray for hip dysplasia.** If your dog seems to be having problems in his hip region, your veterinarian may want to x-ray the dog's hips to see if perhaps he's developed dysplasia. This painful disease can cripple your pet, but with medical advancements today, it can be successfully treated and your pet can continue to live a healthy, pain-free life.

# NOTES

## Tailtip – Healthy Munchies

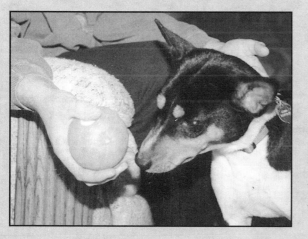

Okay, lets face it. We are all guilty of feeding our dog table scraps at one time or another. Who hasn't let their dog finish off the last drops of milk from the breakfast cereal bowl or snuck a piece of steak down to an eagerly awaiting canine under the table? We all know people food isn't good for dogs, and we all have heard or read that dogs should eat dog food and nothing else. As long as you're feeding your dog a high-quality dog food, he should be getting all the nutrition he needs. It's certainly okay to treat your dog to other goodies, as long as they are healthy treats given in moderation.

Many Basenji owners are delighted to discover that their Basenji loves vegetables — both cooked and raw. For a tasty snack, try giving your Basenji some carrots, green beans, lettuce, squash, or spinach. They also enjoy corn both on and off the cob. Remember, whenever you give your Basenji cooked veggies, make sure they are cooled off first! Of course, fresh veggies should be washed thoroughly to remove any pesticides or dirt that may be on them.

It may come as a surprise to you, but Basenjis also enjoy a great variety of fruits. Try offering green seedless grapes, bananas, watermelon, strawberries, cored apples, and other types of melons to your Basenji. Some Basenjis even enjoy an occasional bite of orange, lemon, or grapefruit! I've known Basenji owners who have put grapes or banana chunks in the freezer — they give these to their Basenjis as frozen treats!

Ice cubes are another treat your Basenji will enjoy crunching on, especially in the summertime. Fill a bowl with ice cubes and watch your Basenji crunch! You can make ice cubes even more fun by freezing dog cookies or biscuits inside them. Just put water and a cookie in a small paper cup. After the treat is frozen, peel away the cup and let your Basenji enjoy!

There are a few vegetables and fruits you shouldn't feed your Basenji. These include cabbage, onions, cucumbers, radishes, raw soybeans, turnips, and avocado. Foods like these, or too much of any people food, may cause digestive upsets in your Basenji. Also, make sure that the fruits you give your Basenji are cored, and that seeds or pits are removed if possible.

Don't try to force your Basenji to try new things — some Basenjis will try new foods willingly, and some don't want any part of them. Just like you, your Basenji has favorites as well as things he finds distasteful. Be patient, keep trying new things, and soon your Basenji will discover that there's a whole world of wonderful tastes and textures out there, and he'll welcome these treats when you offer them.

# NOTES

# Section 14. Rescue Success Stories

*The Secondhand Basenji Handbook* wouldn't be complete if we didn't include some Basenji rescue success stories. We've included stories about folks who have adopted Basenjis, their adoption experiences and their lives with their new Basenjis. You can use Appendix D at the back of this handbook to write your own rescue "success story"!

## *Benji*

Benji's life began in a "puppy mill" somewhere in Missouri. Sold to a broker, he and his sister ended up in a local pet store, where his sister was quickly sold. Benji didn't get so lucky. The pet store sold Benji several times to owners who all returned him for the same reason — his front legs were crooked from spending his whole life inside a crate with a grating floor.

After being returned so many times, the pet store "hid" Benji in the back room, and had a veterinarian put splints on his front legs in an attempt to straighten and strengthen them. They kept him there for a few months, and then sold him at a "deep discount" to a young man who lived in an apartment.

The young man discovered quickly that this energetic Basenji puppy didn't belong in his tiny apartment, and gave him up to his sister, who kept him only a week before she turned him over to the animal shelter. She claimed he wasn't good with her children. So, at only five months old, Benji found himself on death row.

Fortunately for Benji, the staff at the shelter thought he was too pretty and sweet to destroy, and they kept him longer than they normally would have. Benji's salvation came when someone from another rescue organization called and told me there was a Basenji puppy in the shelter, and if someone didn't come to pick him up that Friday afternoon, he would be put to sleep on Saturday morning.

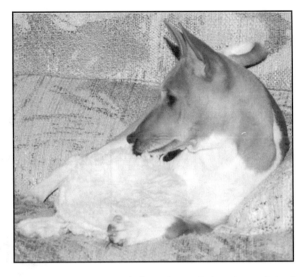

When I arrived at the shelter to rescue Benji, the workers were just getting ready to close up for the evening. They released Benji to me free of charge, and were happy to provide me with all of Benji's paperwork, including several bills of sale and papers indicating where Benji had come from as well as his complete health history. They told me they had kept Benji as long as they could, and they hated the thought of destroying such a sweet little dog.

Benji didn't mind the vet checkup or the bath he received that evening, and after getting a clean bill of health from the vet, he came home to meet the rest of our "pack." We evaluated Benji with children of several ages and found he was simply a normal, playful Basenji who got along fine with children as well as adults.

*The Secondhand Basenji Handbook*

Benji's adopters had always wanted a Basenji, and they claim it was "love at first sight." Benji has lived with them longer than he has ever lived anywhere, and it looks like he's home to stay!

## *Sheba*

Sheba came to rescue as a "displaced" dog. Her owners had their first child, who was at the age where he was just beginning to walk. The baby would crawl up to Sheba, grab hold of whatever he could, and try to lift himself up. He was also very interested in Sheba's toys, and Sheba would growl at him if he came too close. Sheba's owner tearfully explained that they were afraid the dog might hurt the baby, and they felt terrible about leaving her crated most of the time. They had tried everything they could think of the try and get the dog and child to coexist peacefully, but had concluded that the best thing they could do for Sheba was find her a new home.

We were amazed at what accompanied Sheba when she came to live with us at rescue — not only did she come with a leash and collar, but also had her crate, blankets, a wide assortment of toys, and a 40 lb. bag of dog food. Obviously, Sheba was a very well loved and cared for dog. Sheba's owner told me that one of the things she'd miss most about her dog was the fact that Sheba loved to sleep at the foot of the bed, under the covers.

Sheba had lived with us for about a month when she was adopted out. Sheba spent several months in her new home with an older couple. She didn't bother their allergies, was content on their leather furniture, and it seemed that she was home to stay. In fact, she'd even reclaimed her favorite place to sleep — right at the foot of the bed, under the covers.

Unfortunately, after several months in her new home, Sheba began to have health problems that caused her to be ravenously hungry all of the time. She'd try to eat anything remotely edible, and was having behavior problems because of this. In addition, she had begun to lose weight at an alarming rate. Not wanting to deal with the behavioral changes and associated problems of caring for a sick dog, Sheba's adopters returned her to rescue.

The veterinarian was at a loss to explain what was going wrong with Sheba's health, and ran a battery of tests to try and pinpoint the cause of her troubles. Eventually, it was discovered that Sheba had an almost non-functioning pancreas. This meant that she was unable to properly digest the food she ate due to a pancreatic enzyme deficiency. There were two choices for Sheba, then. She either had to be on medication and a special diet for the rest of her life, or she could be put to sleep.

Fortunately, for Sheba, her breeder was able to take the dog back. The daily medications and special diet requirements were a challenge that Sheba's breeder was willing to take on. Under her breeder's love and care, Sheba returned to a normal weight and regained her sweet temperament. Today, Sheba is a healthy, happy Basenji who's found a permanent home with her breeder — who just the other day happened to mention how wonderful it was to have a Basenji again, sleeping under the covers at the foot of the bed.

## Windsor

Windsor was given up by his previous owner because he was destructive and would "fight back" when beaten. Before his first birthday, Windsor had fathered three litters, and he'd been "in jail but bailed out" once. His previous owner even described how Windsor had chewed through the electrical cord on a dryer, but came out of the incident unharmed. When we went to pick up Windsor and take him into rescue, he was chained in the backyard while another Basenji companion of his was allowed to run free. His owner explained that Windsor was chained so that "the two of them wouldn't tear up the yard." From talking on the phone with the owner, I expected a real terror, but what we found instead was exactly the opposite.

Windsor was a beautiful dog with a very thick, full coat of the deepest red color imaginable. He had the mandatory four white feet, white tailtip, and white chest, but other than that there wasn't a spot of white on him anywhere. He was absolutely stunning to behold. His personality was incredibly sweet, and he was gentle and as laid-back as they come. The only thing Windsor left his old home with was one toy and a small coffee can of dog food. His owner explained that the two dogs had shared everything from one crate to one food bowl.

As terribly destructive as Windsor's old owner made him sound, we found him to be completely the opposite. He was a perfect gentleman in the house, and never tried to sample the furniture or any electrical cords. The only time he was destructive was when crated, and then all he would do is shred his blanket. Apparently, Windsor really wasn't used to being in a crate by himself, but with a lot of gentle persistence, he accepted it in time.

It was a long time after her Basenji-mix had died before Janet Onderchanin decided to look for another canine companion, and she found a fantastic companion in Windsor:

> *"I chose a Basenji because they are very unique. There is nothing else quite like them. They can be gentle and affectionate, then be quick and playful. It seems that they can always find ways to get your attention. My first dog, Skippy, was a Basenji-mix. Skippy was with me for almost eleven years, and when he died I really missed his companionship. Once I got over the grief of losing him, I began looking for another dog. Then I found Windsor."*

> *"Windsor is a two-year-old male Basenji that I adopted back in January of 1996. He has become the love of my life, and an absolute joy to be with."*

"Windsor and I have had many adventures, such as walking on the island near my home and going to the park. He loves to watch the geese and ducks, and really enjoys seeing the squirrels. He has even joined me on a trip up north for a weekend getaway. Windsor has many toys and gets a lot of treats, and he loves to play with people."

"Windsor has another companion — the dog at my parents' house. She's a mixed-breed named Muffin, and she's a rescue too."

"Windsor had a rough life before he was rescued, and together we are enjoying a wonderful life together. Thank you for bringing him into my life!"

## *Brandy*

As a puppy, Brandy was a very active, challenging Basenji. She had bounced around from home to home, and was finally turned over to rescue by an owner who had gone through a divorce situation and couldn't take Brandy when she moved.

Brandy was in rough shape when she came to live with us. Her coat was a dusty, washed out red, very short and prickly. The hair around her neck had been worn and broken from having been tied outside for long periods of time, and her nails were so long that they curled under. Her ears were missing hair, and she had scars on her face and a broken tooth — and she was petrified of being hit. If someone so much as raised their hand in the air towards her, she would drop to the ground as low as she could, close her brown eyes tight, and cower and wince, waiting to be punished. It was obvious that she'd been abused, and it was a long time before she'd let anyone pet her on the head and not flinch. With lots of love and care, Brandy grew back a new coat, and the hair came back on her hears. She was a pretty girl even in the sorry state she'd first come to us in, but given time, care and love, she grew absolutely beautiful.

She was very active, and would keep on going long after the other dogs had decided to call it quits. It was this energy level that drew Jim Langeloh and Tina Reese to Brandy. "We lead a very active lifestyle," says Tina. "We go out running every day, and Brandy comes with us. She really seems to enjoy the exercise. Afterwards she will find a sunny spot, usually right on the window seat, and nap."

"She'll get her energy bursts," Jim says. "She'll zoom around for a few seconds, bouncing off of furniture, and being really silly. She also found my raccoon fur hat," he laughs. "I think it's her favorite toy of all."

Brandy has a wide range of tastes. "She loves raw carrots," Tina says. Brandy also loves to munch on strawberries, watermelon, and grapes. And ice cubes. "She's so funny with the ice cubes. She'll bat them around with her paws and watch them slide across the kitchen floor!"

# Appendix A. The Well-Stocked Basenji Library

If you're interested in finding out more about Basenjis, you may want to take a look at some of the books, magazines, and videos listed in this appendix. Here you'll find excellent resources on these "barkless" wonders and on Basenji-related activities. Also included in this appendix are several works of fiction that no Basenji-lover should be without.

You may get lucky and find some of these books at your local bookstore or library. If not, many of the following titles can be ordered by your local bookstore, on the Internet, or directly from the publishers. If the book you're interested in has an ISBN, you'll want to have it handy when you order.

Some privately published and out-of-print titles may be hard to find. Look for these at secondhand bookstores and Basenji-related web sites, or try to find them via Internet book location services.

To get your search for Basenji information on the Internet started, we've included a short list of Internet addresses at the end of this appendix. You can get to many other Basenji-related sites by using the links on the web sites included in this listing or by searching for "Basenji" on any of the major Internet search engines.

We've included publisher contact information for some of the following titles. However, addresses and phone numbers for independently published titles and club-sponsored publications change frequently, so they aren't included here. The latest ordering information for most of the titles in this appendix can be found at the Zande Basenjis (Marvin & Sally Wallis) web site *(http://freepages.pavilion.net/users/zandebas)*. Their listing of Basenji Related Books has contact information that is frequently updated.

# Reference Books

### The Barkless Dog
By B. Bickering, Jr. and R. J. Brach, Exposition-Banner Publications, 1962.

### Basenji, Dog from the Past
By Forrest Bryant Johnson. Limited edition privately published 1971 and 1978. Reprinted in 1993 by A Thousand Autumns Press, 760 Hermosa Palms Avenue, Las Vegas, NV 98123, U.S.A.

### Basenjis — Favourites Among Pharaohs and Hunters in the Jungle
By Helena Strombert and Ing-Marie Hagelin. Although currently available only in Swedish, this book contains many wonderful photographs.

### A Basenji for Me
By Mirrie St. Erme Cardew. Published by Midland Counties Publications, 24 the Hollow, Earl Shilton, Leicester LE9 7NA, England

### The Basenji Illustrated

By Robert W. Cole. Privately published by Robert Cole in 1978.

### The Basenji, Out of Africa to You

By Susan Coe. ISBN 0-944875-02-5. Published in 1990 by Doral Publishing, 8560 SW Salish Lane, Suite 300, Wilsonville, OR 97070-9612, U.S.A. Call toll free (800) 633-5385 or FAX (508) 682-2648.

### The Basenji, Out of Africa to You — A New Look

By Susan Coe. ISBN 0-944875-42-4. Published in 1994 by Doral Publishing, 8560 SW Salish Lane, Suite 300, Wilsonville, OR 97070-9612, U.S.A. Order through book stores or directly from publisher. Call toll free (800) 633-5385 or FAX (508) 682-2648.

### Basenjis

By Jack Shafer & Bob Mankey. ISBN 0-86622-993-0. Published in 1990 by T.F.H. Publications, Inc., 1 T.F.H. Plaza, Third and Union Avenues, Neptune City, New Jersey 07753, U.S.A.

### Basenjis: The Barkless Dogs

By Veronica Tudor-Williams. Also known as "The Red Book." Published in 1946 by James Heap.

### Basenjis: The Barkless Dogs

By Veronica Tudor-Williams. Also known as "The Blue Book." First edition published in 1946; second edition published in 1954. Published by Watmoughs Limited, Idle, Bradford & London. (Revised second edition has different photographs.)

### Basenjis: The Barkless Dogs

By Veronica Tudor-Williams. Also known as "The Rust Book." Published in 1976 by David & Carles.

### The Basenji Stacked and Moving

By Robert Cole. ISBN 0-920939-00-7. An illustrated explanation of the 1954 breed standard. Published in 1987 by Doral Publishing, 8560 SW Salish Lane, Suite 300, Wilsonville, OR 97070-9612, U.S.A. Order through book stores or directly from publisher. Call toll free (800) 633-5385 or FAX (508) 682-2648.

### The Complete Basenji

By Elspet Ford. ISBN 0-87605-016-X. Published in 1993 by Howell Book House, New York, U.S.A. (Also published by Maxwell MacMillan Canada, Inc., Don Mills, Ontario, Canada, and Ringpress Books.)

### A Dingo in the Family

By Gill Rhyorchuk. Published in 1980 by Inkata Press Pty Ltd. ISBN 0-909605-19-x. (Paperback ISBN 0-909605-20-3.) The author has owned Basenjis, Dingoes and a Basenji mix. This book talks about her experiences with both breeds and discusses the differences and similarities between them.

### Fula, Basenji from the Jungle

By Veronica Tudor-Williams. ISBN 0-9513550-0-7. The story of the 1959 search for Basenji puppies in the South Sudan. All profits from this book are donated to charity at the request of the author. Available from *The Basenji* magazine, 789 Linton Hill Road, Newtown, PA 18940, U.S.A.

### How to Raise and Train a Basenji

By Jack Shafer and Bob Mankey. ISBN 0-87666-239-4. Published by T.F.H. Publications, Inc., 1 T.F.H. Plaza, Third and Union Avenues, Neptune City, New Jersey 07753, U.S.A. This title has been re-released several times and is readily found in pet stores.

### Jungle for Sale

By Henry Trefflich. LCCN 67-24653. Published by Hawthorn Books, Inc., New York, U.S.A. The author imported Kindu and Kasenji, and the book contains a section on Basenjis.

### The New Knowledge of Dog Behavior

By Clarence Pfaffenberger. Published in 1963 by Hardback Howell Books. Clarence Pfaffenberger was a member of the Board of Directors of Guide Dogs for the Blind. Inc., of San Rafael, CA. The book is based on the research carried out by the author and by Dr. J. Paul Scott, and it includes photos of Basenjis and Basenji/Cocker Spaniel crosses.

### The Secondhand Basenji Handbook: The Guide to Adopting and Living with a "Rescued" Basenji

By Patrick J. Cotter and Maria Cotter. The second edition (ISBN 0-9658488-1-7) was published in June, 1999 by Windigo, P.O. Box 183176, Shelby Twp., MI 48318-3176, U.S.A. Available from your favorite bookseller, or order directly from Windigo using the order form at the back of this handbook. The first edition, published in July, 1996 (ISBN 0-9658488-0-9) is out of print. Quantity discounts available to rescue groups and breed clubs that support Basenji rescue.

*The Secondhand Basenji Handbook*

**So You Want to Breed Your Basenji**
**So You Want to Buy a Basenji**
**So You Want to Course Your Basenji**
**So You Want to Enjoy Your Basenji**
Privately published by Mary Lou Kenworthy.

**Tips on Raising Your Basenji**
Privately published by Betsy Polglase.

**Understanding the Practical Application of Genetics**
By Mary Lou Kenworthy.

**Where Have All the Old Dogs Gone?**
By Carmella Troisi-Hoerr, Mary Lou Kenworthy & Karen Butler.

**Why a Basenji?**
By Ron Thackerah. Published by English Publications.

**Your Basenji**
By Evelyn Green. Published in 1976 by Denlinger's Publishing, Ltd., P.O. Box 76, Fairfax, VA 22030, U.S.A.

**Your Basenji Puppy**
By Marie Steele and Barbara Field.

# Fiction, Poetry and Craft Books

### August Magic: A Novel
By Veronica Anne Starbuck. ISBN 0-9658488-2-5, LCCN 98-90577. Published in September 1998 by Windigo, P.O. Box 183176, Shelby Twp., MI 48318-3176, U.S.A. Available from your favorite bookseller, or order directly from Windigo (see the order form at the back of this handbook). A novel "about second chances, about the magic that people and companion animals can make together, and about how saving a life can have a positive effect on your own."

### Basenji Fever
By A. C. Dehass. Published in 1980 by Arthur H. Stockwell Limited. This is a small paperback book of poems.

### Basenjis Charted for Counted Cross-Stitch
Privately published by Carmella Troisi-Hoerr in 1987.

### Basenjis — Love Laughter and Tears
By Ann Cooper. This is a book of poems about Basenjis. Privately published.

### Binti, Adventures With a Basenji
By Catherine Ritlaw.

### Call of the Marsh
By Jill Wylie. Published in 1979 by Rhodesian Publishing Co.

### Candle, A Story of Love and Faith

By Sally Ann Smith. ISBN 0-944875-22-X. A colorfully illustrated Christmas fable. Published in 1991 by Doral Publishing, 8560 SW Salish Lane, Suite 300, Wilsonville, OR 97070-9612, U.S.A. Order through book stores or directly from publisher. Call toll free (800) 633-5385 or FAX (508) 682-2648.

### Canis Basenji

By Robert Vavra. A cartoon book about life with Basenjis. Available through the Basenji Club of America.

### A Christmas Fable

By Andie Paysinger. Published in 1989.

### Curly Tails and Other Basenji Nonsense

By Susan Coe.

### The Dogs of Our Lives

Compiled by Louise Goodyear Murray. ISBN 1-55972-289-4. A Birch Lane Press Book. Published by Carol Publishing Group. Includes three stories by Sally Ann Smith, "The Chance of a Lifetime," "The Legend of the Littlest Basenji" and "The Dog at Night."

### The Dog with a Bad Name
By K. D. Nason.

### Good-bye, My Lady
By James Street. ISBN 0-67142-890-X. Published by Peoples Book Club and J. B. Lippincott Co.

### Walk My Way
By Paige Dixon. Published in 1980 by Athenaeum Press. This is the story of "Kitty," a 14 year old girl hiking into the wilderness of New Hampshire. She's joined by a Basenji who was lost in a car accident, and later by an elderly man and his young grandson.

### Yodels, Wails and Basenji Tails
Edited by Angela Anderson and Pam Maremont. Published in 1998. A compilation of Basenji stories. Proceeds are to be used to fund Basenji rescue.

### Zende, a Dog of a Very Special Breed
Privately published by Margaret Christy Davies. The six stories in this book were published in *The Basenji* magazine in 1968/69.

# Club-Sponsored Publications

### African Stock Project
Compiled by Susan Coe and sponsored by the Basenji Club of America. Published in September 1998 it is an ongoing project. The book will be reprinted with additional information and photos, updates, and corrections as new information becomes available.

### At Home with Basenjis
Published by the Basenji Club of Southeastern Wisconsin (U.S.A.). This book covers many aspects of Basenji ownership, including items on history, traits, training and care.

### The Basenji — A Handbook
Issued in 1958 by the Basenji Owners & Breeders Association (England).

### The Basenji in New South Wales 1968-1993
Various authors. Published by the Basenji Club of New South Wales (Australia) in 1993. A history of the Basenji Club of New South Wales. A 25th anniversary publication.

### Basenji Klub Deutschland — 1977-1997
Edited by Uschi Grewe. Published by the Klub to coincide with the 20th Anniversary Championship Show. Twenty years of Basenjis in Germany are celebrated in this book.

### Basenji Owner's Manual
Published by Evergreen Basenji Club (U.S.A.) members & friends of Basenjis.

**Basenji Owners & Breeders Association Handbook 1995-1996**

Published by the Basenji Owners & Breeders Association (England) in March 1997.

**Basenji Owners & Breeders Association Handbook 1997-1998**

Published by the Basenji Owners & Breeders Association (England) in March 1999.

**The Basenji Yearbook 1992**

Published by the Northern Basenji Society (England).

**Magnolia Basenji Club Handbook**

Published in 1971, and now out of print.

**A Review of the Basenji Standard**

Editing and layout by Susan Coe and Sandra Bridges. Published in January, 1991. 12-page fold-out brochure of the official Basenji Club of America Basenji standard with comments. Available through the Basenji Club of America.

**Verses and Curses**

Poetry by various authors. Published by the Basenji Club of Victoria.

# Independent Basenji Periodicals

**The Basenji**

Published monthly by Jon and Susan Coe. 789 Linton Hill Road, Newton, PA 18940, U.S.A.

# Periodicals Issued in Conjunction with Basenji Club Memberships

### The Bark

Monthly newsletter of The Basenji Club of Northern California, U.S.A.

### Basenjibladet

Basenji Magazine (Sweden).

### Basenji Chronicle

Newsletter published three times a year by the Basenji Club of Great Britain.

### Basenji Club of Canada

Newsletter.

### Basenji Club of Greater Detroit

Newsletter (U.S.A.).

### Basenji Club of Southern California

Newsletter.

### Basenji Companions

Bi-monthly newsletter of The Basenji Companions (U.S.A.), a club dedicated to pet Basenjis.

**Basenji Enthusiasts Club of South Australia**
Newsletter.

**Basenji News**
Newsletter of the Basenji Club of New South Wales (Australia).

**Basenji News**
Quarterly newsletter of the Bay State Basenji Club (U.S.A.).

**Basenji Owners And Breeders Association (BOBA)**
Newsletter published every six months (England).

**Bulletin**
Glossy quarterly magazine published by the Basenji Club of America.

**Bulletin Board Newsletter**
Newsletter published eight times a year by the Basenji Club of America.

**Buschtrommel**
Newsletter of the Basenjiklub Deutschland (Germany).

**Curly Tails**
Monthly newsletter of the Hoosier Basenji Club (U.S.A.).

# Basenji Pedigree Books

### The Basenji (A'Asia) 1947-1976

Published by the Basenji Hound Club of New South Wales (Australia) and the Basenji Club of Victoria (Australia).

### The Basenji (A'Asia) 1976-1981

Published by the Basenji Hound Club of New South Wales (Australia).

### The Basenji (A'Asia) 1981-1989

Published by the Basenji Hound Club of New South Wales (Australia).

### Basenji Champions, 1937-1977

Edited by Jayne Wilson-Stringer & Elspet Ford. Published in March, 1978 by Theddlethorpe All Saints, Lincs., England. A historical record of Basenji champions in England.

### Basenji Champions, 1978-1989

Edited by Jayne Wilson-Stringer. Published in April, 1990 by Theddlethorpe All Saints, Lincs., England. A historical record of Basenji champions in England.

### Basenji Champions, 1990-1996
Edited by Jayne Wilson-Stringer. Published in April, 1990 by Theddlethorpe All Saints, Lincs., England. A historical record of Basenji champions in England.

### Basenji Champions: 1982/86
Published in 1988 by Camino E. E. & B. Co.

### Basenji Champions of Sweden, 1951-1996
Edited by Mia Lowbeer and Lotten Fornell. A historical record of Basenji champions in Sweden.

### Basenjis in Australia
Published by the Basenji Club of New South Wales (Australia).

### Finnish Champion/Pedigree Book
Published in 1991 by the Finnish Basenji Club.

### The Years of the American Basenji
Compiled by Susan Coe, Melody Russell and L. Jane Williams. The historic Basenji pedigree book, including over 2,000 American titled Basenjis from the first American Basenjis to present.

# Basenjis in Movies and Videos

### Ace Ventura: Pet Detective
1994. Jim Carrey. New release of this film on video includes footage of a black and white Basenji, which was cut from the original release. This Basenji was featured on the cover of the video in Australia.

### African Queen
Humphrey Bogart; Catherine Hepburn. Basenji sitting on lap of native in church scene at the beginning of the movie.

### All's Quiet on the Canine Front (1930)
### Foreign Agent (ca. 1930-35)
### Trader Horn (ca. 1930-35)
Movie shorts of about five minutes each from the "Dogville" comedy series made by Metro Goldwyn Meyer studios in the U.S. during the early 1930's. Contains trained dogs as actors — two of whom are clearly Basenjis and may be the two Basenji dogs that Errol Flynn picked up in his safari to the Belgian Congo.

### The American Kennel Club Basenji Standard Video
Video code #VVT 402. Available from the AKC/ Video Fulfillment, 5580 Centerview Drive, Suite 200, Raleigh, NC 27606, U.S.A. Call (919) 233-9780 or fax (919) 233-3627.

### Good-bye, My Lady

Walter Brennan; Brandon de Wilde; Sidney Poitier. Screenplay from the book by James Street. Filmed in Louisiana in the 1950's. Black and white. Warner's Home Video Family Classic.

### The Magic of Lassie

1978. James Stewart; Alice Faye. During one of the scenes, a Basenji can be seen in the cab of an 18-wheeler in the parking lot. The scene only lasts for a short time, but the cab window and the Basenji take up the full screen.

### Mystic Fire Video, Inc.

Possibly the fourth (and last) volume contains the Borneo Basenji.

### Ring of Fire

1988. Lorne & Lawrence Blair Production.

### Zaire '87-'88

Edited from two trips to northeastern Zaire by Basenji breeders. Seventy minutes. Available from Kibushi Kennels, 8761 N. Reams Rd., Centralia, MO 65240, U.S.A.

# Basenjis Mentioned in Books, Magazines, Periodicals and Research

### The African Giant
By Stuart Cloete.

### All About Dogs
By Carol Burger. Published in 1962.

### Among Congo Pygmies
By Paul Schebesta. Published in 1993 by Hutchinson & Co.

### Ancient History of the Basenjis
By Captain F. B. Johnson. Published in 1971.

### Animals of East Africa
By Louis B. Leakey. Published in 1969.

### Basic Colored Pencil Techniques
By Bet Borgeson. ISBN 0891347364. Published by North Light Books, Cincinnati, Ohio, U.S.A. Opposite the title page there's a picture called "Travelers" showing two tri-colored Basenjis on a trail in a wooded area.

### Chad
By Stephen A. Tring. Published in 1966 by Reindeer Books. Children's fiction.

### Charted Egyptian Designs
A Dover publication. Includes a stylized Basenji.

### Children of the Forest: Life with the Mbuti Pygmies
By Kevin Duffy. ISBN 0-7090-2559-9. Published in 1984 by Robert Hale, Limited, London, England.

### Claud Cockburn Sums Up
ISBN 0 7043 3468 2. Published by Quartet Books of London, Melbourne & New York.

### The Coloured Peacock
By Ruth Kendell. A collection of short stories which features a story called "Paperwork" that mentions Basenjis.

### Congo Kitabu
By Jean Pierre Hallet. Published in 1966 by Random Press.

### Country Life (May 21, 1992 Issue)
A periodical published in England. Contains a photograph of two brindle Basenjis in a quarantine kennel.

### Debylandt's Dogs of All Nations
Published in 1904. Includes "Terrier du Congo Belge."

### The Dingo in Australia and Asia
By Professor Laurie Corbett. ISBN 0-8014-8264-X. Published in 1995 by Cornell University Press.

### Dog Fancy (June, 1991 Issue)

A periodical published in the U.S.A. Includes the Breed Profile "Out of Africa" by Sally Ann Smith and a centerfold photograph.

### Dog Locomotion & Gait Analysis

By Curtis M. Brown. Published by Hoflin Publishing, U.S.A.

### Dog Problems: The Gentle, Modern Cure

By David Weston & Ruth Ross. ISBN 0876055072. Published in December, 1993 by Howell Book House. Basenjis are used in illustrations, and a couple of references are included.

### Dog World (July, 1994 Issue)

A periodical published in the U.S.A. Includes "The Barkless Dogs of Africa" by Barbara Eastwood, and "Cassie's Boomerang Pups" by Sally Ann Smith.

### The Domestic Dog: Its Evolution, Behavior and Interactions with People

Edited by James Serpell. ISBN 0 521 41529 2 (hard cover) and 0 521 42537 9 (paperback). Published in 1995 by Cambridge University Press.

### A Donkey and a Dandelion

By Doris Rybot with illustrations by Douglas Hall. Fiction. Published in 1966 by Hutchinson, London, England.

### Fabulous Congo

By Felice Belloti. Published in 1954 by Andrew Dakers, Ltd.

### Facing Danger in the Last Wilderness
Published in 1962 by Bolton House, Inc.

### Figure of Eight
By Patricia Cockburn. Published by Chatto & Windus, Hogarth Press. The author tells how the Basenji Amataganzig came to London, her escapades there, and how she went to live with Veronica Tudor-Williams.

### Genetics and the Social Behavior of the Dog
By John Paul Scott and John L. Fuller. Published in 1965 by University of Chicago Press. Covers 13 years of breeding and cross-breeding five breeds of dogs — including Basenjis — while testing the offspring for genetic traits of behavior.

### Hunting Dogs in America
By Jeff Griffen. Illustrated by Raymond S. Pease. Published in 1964. Includes a line drawing of two Basenjis near an antelope with a hunter holding a spear in the background and a photograph of Ch. Coptokin Ameliette.

### Im Herzen von Afrika
By Dr. Schweinfurth. Published in 1918.

### In Praise of Dogs
By Tara Darling and Kathy Darling. Includes photographs of Basenjis.

### In the Shade of the Tree
By Piers Anthony. A science fiction story with two Basenjis in it.

### The Kennel Club's Illustrated Breed Standards: The Official Guide to Registered Breeds

Published in 1998 by Ebury Press, London, England. The list of Illustrations features: "Fula of the Congo," a pastel drawing by Andie Paysinger done in 1975.

### Kennel Gazette (May, 1984 Issue)

A periodical published in England. Includes "Hunting Dogs of the Mediterranean" by David Hancock. Features a photograph of Bokoto Nile Arabis of Drakesleat.

### Kennel Gazette (June, 1996 Issue)

A periodical published in England. Contains an article on Basenjis.

### Land and People of the Kasai

By Hilton Simpson.

### Leighton's New Book of the Dog

Published in 1906. Includes a section on Basenjis.

### Leopard in My Lap

By Michaela Denis. Published in 1955 by Julia Messner, Inc.

### Love Is a Many Splendored Thing

By Han Suyin. Two Basenjis are mentioned.

**Man's Best Friend: National Geographic Book of Dogs**
1958 & 1966.

**My Pygmy and Negro Hosts**
By Paul Schbesta. Published in 1955 by Hutchinson & Co.

**National Geographic (October, 1937 Issue)**
A periodical published in U.S.A. Includes a picture of the three African Basenji Imports shown at Cruft's dog show in London, during February, 1937.

**The Natural History of Dogs**
By Richard and Alice Fiennes. Published in 1970 for the America Museum of Natural History by Natural History Press.

**Once upon a Time in Egypt**
By Frances Kent Gere. Published in 1937.

**Saturday Evening Post (December 6, 1941 Issue)**
A periodical published in U.S.A. Includes "Please Come Home My Lady" by James W. Street.

**Tarzan of the Apes**
Comic book. Gold Key "Collector's Edition" #195. Published in September, 1970 by Western Publishing Co., Inc., Poughkeepsie, New York 10012, U.S.A. At the end of the comic are four pages "reprinted by popular demand" of "Bantu, Dog of the Arande" (copyright 1966, Western Publishing Co., Inc.). It is an accurate story about Bantu, a Basenji.

### Tea Shop Walks in Lancashire
By Clive Price. Published in 1997. The picture on page 116 shows a Basenji outside The Priory, Scorton.

### Teen Age Dog Stories
Edited by David Thomas. Published in 1949. Includes "Please Come Home My Lady" by James Street.

### This Dog for Hire
By Carol Lea Benjamin. ISBN 0-8027-3292-5. Published in 1996 by Walker and Co., New York, U.S.A. A Basenji is one of the characters.

### The Unicorns of Kilimanjaro
By Robert Vavra. Published in 1988 by William Morrow and Co., Inc., New York, U.S.A. This book is full of Robert Vavra's photographs, including himself and his Basenjis; also a sketch of a Basenji. Also includes references to his Basenjis and Veronica Tudor Williams in the text.

### Wild Dogs of the World
By Lois E. Bueler. Published in 1973 by Stein & Day (U.S.A.). ISBN 0-8128-1568-6, and Saunders of Toronto, Ltd. (Canada).

# Basenjis on the Internet

### Basenji Club of America
*http://www.basenji.org*

### Basenji Companions
*http://www.ultranet.com/~basenji/*
Basenji Companions is an international club devoted to pet Basenjis and their owners. Members of the club can participate in the Basenji Companions electronic mailing list.

### Basenji-L
Electronic mailing list. To subscribe to Basenji-L, send e-mail to: *LISTSERV@APPLE.EASE.LSOFT.COM*
In the body of the message include the single line: *SUBSCRIBE Basenji-L Firstname Lastname*
Include your First and Last name when subscribing (not the words "Firstname" and "Lastname").

### Basenji Rescue and Transport, Inc. Web Site
*http://basenjirescue.org*

### Basenji Underground Railroad Web Site
*http://midtown.net/bur*

# NOTES

# *Appendix B. Rescue Contact Log*

Use the forms on the following pages as a place to keep track of the rescue people and groups you contact.

# Rescue Contact #1

DATE:

PERSON CONTACTED:

PHONE NUMBER:

RESCUES AVAILABLE? YES NO

INFORMATION ABOUT RESCUES AVAILABLE:
Name:

Age

Color:

Adoption Application and Contract Requested? YES NO

NOTES:

RESCUE ORGANIZATION:

LEFT MESSAGE? YES NO

DATE CALL RETURNED:

Sex:

Spayed/Neutered? YES NO

# Rescue Contact #2

DATE:

PERSON CONTACTED:

PHONE NUMBER:

RESCUES AVAILABLE? YES NO

INFORMATION ABOUT RESCUES AVAILABLE:
Name:

Age

Color:

Adoption Application and Contract Requested? YES NO

NOTES:

RESCUE ORGANIZATION:

LEFT MESSAGE? YES NO

DATE CALL RETURNED:

Sex:

Spayed/Neutered? YES NO

## Rescue Contact #3

DATE:                                              RESCUE ORGANIZATION:

PERSON CONTACTED:                    LEFT MESSAGE? YES NO

PHONE NUMBER:                            DATE CALL RETURNED:

RESCUES AVAILABLE? YES NO

INFORMATION ABOUT RESCUES AVAILABLE:
Name:                                                  Sex:

Age                                                      Spayed/Neutered? YES NO

Color:

Adoption Application and Contract Requested? YES NO

NOTES:

# Rescue Contact #4

DATE:                                          RESCUE ORGANIZATION:

PERSON CONTACTED:                   LEFT MESSAGE? YES NO

PHONE NUMBER:                          DATE CALL RETURNED:

RESCUES AVAILABLE? YES NO

INFORMATION ABOUT RESCUES AVAILABLE:
Name:                                          Sex:

Age                                            Spayed/Neutered? YES NO

Color:

Adoption Application and Contract Requested? YES NO

NOTES:

## Rescue Contact #5

DATE:

RESCUE ORGANIZATION:

PERSON CONTACTED:

LEFT MESSAGE? YES NO

PHONE NUMBER:

DATE CALL RETURNED:

RESCUES AVAILABLE? YES NO

INFORMATION ABOUT RESCUES AVAILABLE:

Name:

Sex:

Age

Spayed/Neutered? YES NO

Color:

Adoption Application and Contract Requested? YES NO

NOTES:

# Rescue Contact #6

DATE:                                            RESCUE ORGANIZATION:

PERSON CONTACTED:                    LEFT MESSAGE? YES NO

PHONE NUMBER:                           DATE CALL RETURNED:

RESCUES AVAILABLE? YES NO

INFORMATION ABOUT RESCUES AVAILABLE:
Name:                                            Sex:

Age                                               Spayed/Neutered? YES NO

Color:

Adoption Application and Contract Requested? YES NO

NOTES:

## Rescue Contact #7

DATE:

PERSON CONTACTED:

PHONE NUMBER:

RESCUES AVAILABLE? YES NO

INFORMATION ABOUT RESCUES AVAILABLE:
Name:

Age

Color:

RESCUE ORGANIZATION:

LEFT MESSAGE? YES NO

DATE CALL RETURNED:

Sex:

Spayed/Neutered? YES NO

Adoption Application and Contract Requested? YES NO

NOTES:

# Rescue Contact #8

DATE:

RESCUE ORGANIZATION:

PERSON CONTACTED:

LEFT MESSAGE? YES NO

PHONE NUMBER:

DATE CALL RETURNED:

RESCUES AVAILABLE? YES NO

INFORMATION ABOUT RESCUES AVAILABLE:
Name:

Sex:

Age

Spayed/Neutered? YES NO

Color:

Adoption Application and Contract Requested? YES NO

NOTES:

## Rescue Contact #9

DATE:

PERSON CONTACTED:

PHONE NUMBER:

RESCUES AVAILABLE? YES NO

INFORMATION ABOUT RESCUES AVAILABLE:
Name:

Age

Color:

Adoption Application and Contract Requested? YES NO

NOTES:

RESCUE ORGANIZATION:

LEFT MESSAGE? YES NO

DATE CALL RETURNED:

Sex:

Spayed/Neutered? YES NO

# *Appendix C. Shopping for Your Rescue Basenji: Shopping Lists*

Here are two copies of the shopping list from Section 8, "Planning and Preparing for the New Arrival." We've provided these here so that you can remove a shopping list from this book and take it with you when you go out to shop for your new rescue Basenji.

## Shopping List — Rescue Basenji

☐ Wire crate — A good wire crate size is about 30" L x 22" W x 25" H (76 cm x 56 cm x 64 cm).

☐ Travel crate *or* safety restraint harness for trips in the car — A good travel crate size is 27" L x 20" W x 19" H (69 cm x 51 cm x 48 cm); but for large Basenjis or for long trips consider the 32" L x 23" W x 23" H size (81 cm x 58 cm x 58 cm).

☐ Blankets, bed, or carpeting for crates — Ask the rescue person if the Basenji will tolerate a "doggy bed" in its crate, or if blankets or carpeting is a better idea. (Some carpeting stores will sell or give you extra carpeting samples.)

☐ Food and water dishes for inside the crate — Stainless steel is preferred.

☐ Water dish for outside the crate — Stainless steel is preferred.

☐ Collar — A good nylon or leather buckle-style collar is recommended.

☐ 6-foot (1.8 m) leash — Nylon, cotton, or leather.

☐ Retractable leash — The Flexi® 3-8, 26 foot (8 m) long, is a good one.

☐ Dog license — Remember to bring a rabies vaccination certificate and proof of spay/neuter.

☐ Identification tag — Include your name, address, city, state, phone number with area code, and the phone number to your dog's tattoo or microchip registry, and indicate that your dog is tattooed or microchipped.

☐ Plastic-coated metal wire tie out, if necessary (Something that can't easily be chewed through.)

☐ Food _____(Note brand/type that dog is currently being fed.)

☐ Vitamins _____(Note brand/type that dog is currently being given.)

☐ Treats _____(Note brand/type that dog is currently being fed. If you choose rawhide, look for rawhide made in the USA.)

☐ Chew toys, such as Nylabones®, Gumabones®, Kong® toys, etc.

☐ "Fetch" toys, such as a rope toy or fake sheepskin toy

☐ Bitter Apple® spray (If necessary to discourage chewing on houseplants and furniture.)

☐ Stain/Odor remover (Accidents do happen!)

☐ Nail clippers (If you plan to trim the dog's nails yourself.)

☐ Grooming brush, stripping comb, or hound glove

☐ Gentle pet shampoo

☐ Flea control/Heartworm preventative products — Discuss with the rescue person and your veterinarian.

☐ First aid kit for dogs

☐ Pooper scooper

☐ Magnetic latches for doggy-level cabinets

☐ Film (You'll want to take lots of pictures!)

Additional items not listed here:

## Shopping List — Rescue Basenji

☐ Wire crate — A good wire crate size is about 30" L x 22" W x 25" H (76 cm x 56 cm x 64 cm).

☐ Travel crate *or* safety restraint harness for trips in the car — A good travel crate size is 27" L x 20" W x 19" H (69 cm x 51 cm x 48 cm); but for large Basenjis or for long trips consider the 32" L x 23" W x 23" H size (81 cm x 58 cm x 58 cm).

☐ Blankets, bed, or carpeting for crates — Ask the rescue person if the Basenji will tolerate a "doggy bed" in its crate, or if blankets or carpeting is a better idea. (Some carpeting stores will sell or give you extra carpeting samples.)

☐ Food and water dishes for inside the crate — Stainless steel is preferred.

☐ Water dish for outside the crate — Stainless steel is preferred.

☐ Collar — A good nylon or leather buckle-style collar is recommended.

☐ 6-foot (1.8 m) leash — Nylon, cotton, or leather.

☐ Retractable leash — The Flexi® 3-8, 26 foot (8 m) long, is a good one.

☐ Dog license — Remember to bring a rabies vaccination certificate and proof of spay/neuter.

☐ Identification tag — Include your name, address, city, state, phone number with area code, and the phone number to your dog's tattoo or microchip registry, and indicate that your dog is tattooed or microchipped.

☐ Plastic-coated metal wire tie out, if necessary (Something that can't easily be chewed through.)

☐ Food _____(Note brand/type that dog is currently being fed.)

☐ Vitamins _____(Note brand/type that dog is currently being given.)

☐ Treats _____(Note brand/type that dog is currently being fed. If you choose rawhide, look for rawhide made in the USA.)

☐ Chew toys, such as Nylabones®, Gumabones®, Kong® toys, etc.

☐ "Fetch" toys, such as a rope toy or fake sheepskin toy

☐ Bitter Apple® spray (If necessary to discourage chewing on houseplants and furniture.)

☐ Stain/Odor remover (Accidents do happen!)

☐ Nail clippers (If you plan to trim the dog's nails yourself.)

☐ Grooming brush, stripping comb, or hound glove

☐ Gentle pet shampoo

☐ Flea control/Heartworm preventative products — Discuss with the rescue person and your veterinarian.

☐ First aid kit for dogs

☐ Pooper scooper

☐ Magnetic latches for doggy-level cabinets

☐ Film (You'll want to take lots of pictures!)

Additional items not listed here:

# NOTES

## *Appendix D. My Rescue Basenji Information Sheet*

The following pages are provided so that you can keep information on your rescue Basenji (or Basenjis!) in a handy place. It's a good idea to also keep your veterinarian's phone number in an easy-to find place (such as this book) in case of emergency.

# My Rescue Basenji

Name:

Date of birth (if known):

Age (if known):

Sex:

Date spayed/neutered:

Color:

Weight:

Height:

Date adopted:

Adopted from:

Phone number of rescue contact:

Tattoo/microchip implant number:

Tattoo/microchip implant registered with:

Phone number of tattoo/microchip implant registry:

Unusual markings/scars:

Veterinarian:

Veterinarian phone number:

Special needs?:

The history of my rescue Basenji, and how my rescue Basenji came to live with me:

Place photo here

# My Rescue Basenji

Name:

Date of birth (if known):

Age (if known):

Sex:

Date spayed/neutered:

Color:

Weight:

Height:

Date adopted:

Adopted from:

Phone number of rescue contact:

Tattoo/microchip implant number:

Tattoo/microchip implant registered with:

Phone number of tattoo/microchip implant registry:

Unusual markings/scars:

Veterinarian:

Veterinarian phone number:

Special needs?:

The history of my rescue Basenji, and how my rescue Basenji came to live with me:

Place photo here

# Index

## A

## B

# O

Obedience Training, 57, 129, 152
Off Leash, 7
Older or Younger Dog, 47
Organizations, 25
Other Pets, 44
Outdoors, 8
Overweight, 174

# P

Pedigree Books, 205
Periodicals on or Featuring Basenjis, 205
Pickup Truck Safety, 113, 115
Planning and Preparing for the New Arrival, 103, 117
Policy on Spaying and Neutering, 55, 72
Policy on Taking Dogs Back, 61, 72
Pools and Dogs, 112
Possessiveness, 160

Post-Adoption Follow Up, 60
Preparing for the New Arrival, 103
Problems with Basenjis, 159
Protecting Your Home and Furnishings, 108
Protectiveness, 160
Publications on or Featuring Basenjis, 205
Puppies, 4

# Q

Questions and Answers About Basenjis, 1
Questions You May Be Asked, 33
Questions You Should Ask, 33, 50

# R

Reference Books, 205
Registration Papers, 54
Removing Sticky Substances from Your Dog's Coat, 182

# W

# Y

# Also Available from Windigo . . .

Not since James Street wrote the classic *Good-bye, My Lady* over 40 years ago has a novel about a Basenji come into being with such far-reaching appeal. While Street's "Lady" typified the Basenji of his time (a fairly rare, relatively unknown breed), *August Magic*'s "Ch. Windswept of Hatteras" (a.k.a. "Magic") speaks up for the dogs of our times — both purebred and mix-bred — who find themselves at the mercy of our fast-paced, throw-away society

"*August Magic* is about second chances, about the magic that people and companion animals can make together, and about how saving a life can have a positive effect on your own," says author Veronica Anne Starbuck. A lonely young teacher and a dog in his autumn years find each other and set out on a journey to the wild and beautiful Outer Banks of North Carolina. Along the way, they learn about each other, about the magic of love and trust that is as much a part of life as living and breathing, and about the bittersweet victory in setting painful memories free.

ISBN 0-9658488-2-5

Check with your favorite bookseller or use the order form on the next page to order *August Magic* directly from Windigo for $12.95 (U.S. funds only), plus tax (if applicable) and shipping & handling. Also available online from the Windigo web site at **http://www.windigo.net**.

# Want to order *August Magic* or additional copies of *The Secondhand Basenji Handbook*?

Check with your favorite bookseller or order directly from Windigo via regular mail or the Internet!

| ISBN | Quantity | Description | Price Each (U.S. Funds) | Total |
|---|---|---|---|---|
| 0-9658488-2-5 | | *August Magic: A Novel* by V. A. Starbuck | $12.95 | |
| 0-9658488-1-7 | | *The Secondhand Basenji Handbook* by Patrick J. Cotter & Maria Cotter | $12.00 | |
| | | Shipping and Handling Charge (See information below.) | | |
| | | For deliveries in Michigan, add 6% sales tax | | |
| | | TOTAL (Check or money order payable in U.S. funds only, please.) | | |

**All prices are subject to change. Contact Windigo for latest pricing, quantity discounts, and availability.**

**Mail To:** Windigo
P.O. Box 183176
Shelby Township, MI 48318-3176

**E-mail:** info@windigo.net

**Order online at:** http://www.windigo.net

**Shipping and Handling Charges (U.S.):**
- For orders up to $20.00, add $3.20.
- For orders from $20.01 to $40.00, add $5.00.
- For orders from $40.01 to $60.00, add $7.00.
- For orders over $60.00, add $9.00.

For shipments to North American locations outside of the U.S., please **add $2.00** to the regular shipping charge.

For shipments to locations outside of North America, **add $6.00** to the regular shipping charge.